Spirit of Singing

Songs for building community

Edited by Mardi Tindal and Kate Middleton

Wood Lake
Books

Editors: Kate Middleton and Mardi Tindal
Cover design: Lois Huey-Heck
Music typesetting: Brian Kai
Text editing: Jim Taylor
Music editing: Alan Whitmore
Copyright research: Lindy Jones

We thank the owners and copyright holders for their cooperation in making the publication of this book possible. Specific credit will be found with each song.

A number of the songs included in this selection are traditional, anonymous or in public domain – that is, any copyright that once existed has expired. For these songs, no specific credit has been given. We caution users of this songbook against assuming that they make use of any of these songs without requiring permission; while the melody line may be free of copyright restrictions, the arrangement of chords and other notes is almost always copyrighted, as is the presentation on the page. For example, users may not photocopy pages from this book without permission – even though the words and melody may be in public domain, the physical presentation is copyrighted by the publisher.

We have made every effort, over a period of more than two years, to track all owners and copyright holders. If we have omitted any legitimate owners or copyright holders, we sincerely apologize. We will include the appropriate credit in future editions and reprints of the songbook, and will make royalty payments on the same basis as was offered to other copyright holders.

Canadian Cataloguing in Publication Data
Main entry under title:
Spirit of Singing

Includes index.
ISBN 0-929032-85-3

1. Camping – Songs and music. 2. Songs, English – Canada. I. Tindal, Mardi. II. Middleton, Kate.
M1977.C3S64 1994   782.5'42   C94-910219-9

Reprinted - April 1997, June 1999

Published by Wood Lake Books Inc.
9025 Jim Bailey Road, Kelowna, BC, Canada V4V 1R2

Printed in Canada by
Hignell Printing
Winnipeg

Contents

Dedication

This book is dedicated to N. Bruce McLeod, in celebration of his forty years of ministry, a ministry that has touched us and many others through his love of music and song. It is also offered in loving memory of Sylvia Dunstan, for the wonderful gift of music she has left to us, and of Stanley Middleton, who was guided by a love of music all his life.

Acknowledgments

It should come as no surprise that a book that includes the word "community" in its sub-title will have a number of people to thank. Many thanks go to the enthusiastic congregation of Bellefair United Church. Additional thanks go to Elizabeth Shorten for her tasteful selections; to Pat Agnew, Sharon Aylsworth, Maureen Mealey, Janice Thorne, Annette Taylor, and Bill Conklin for their helpful suggestions; to the choir of Bellefair and their organist and director, Dean Perry, for support and assistance. David Hallman provided invaluable help by providing a number of old songbooks. And without Mary Casey and the library of Camp Big Canoe, and Lindy Jones at Wood Lake Books, we would never have been able to resolve the mysteries of some songs' origins. Finally, thanks to Jim Taylor for his cheerful encouragement and support throughout the process of putting this book together.

Introduction

Kate Middleton and I first met around the campfire at a church camp. We were in our mid-teens at the time, delighted to discover that we knew some of the same camp songs and equally thrilled with the chance to learn new ones from one another. That summer, we shared many spirit-filled hours singing with friends of our own age and with the younger ones who were learning to lead.

The spirit that we discovered and enjoyed there has kept rekindling our friendship through the many years since. And we've come to understand that singing together brought us to that spirit.

A few years ago I returned to directing summer camp and was surprised that there seemed to be so little singing around the campfire, and a very limited repertoire. One day several of my staff came to see me, dusting off a relic they had found in the back of a dresser drawer—an old camp songbook. They liked the words, but they had never heard the songs sung.

"Do you know any of these?" they asked.

Deep into the night, we sang, and they learned, those lovely old pieces— songs that had been locked inside me since those days of singing with Kate.

As we sang together, I realized how much these songs had shaped me, without me knowing it. The teenagers who sang with me couldn't get over how great these old tunes were, and asked me at each campfire that summer to lead them in singing, so that they could lock them into their hearts as well.

I've seen the same thing happen in church and community groups. People struggle with agendas and issues. Sometimes they have difficulty sustaining discussion and conversation, and sometimes they actually generate hostilities. But if someone starts playing a few of their old favorite songs on the piano, they find themselves drawn together and singing along. The music, quite literally, creates harmony.

This is one of the reasons we prepared this book. We want to help people keep the spirit of singing alive in these important gatherings and places along our life journeys.

For Kate and me, it's been renewing to sing the good old songs once more, and to learn new ones, while putting this book together for you. This collection is a mixture of what some might call "sacred" and "secular" music. They don't often get the chance to live together in print. Most secular publishers are scared of including anything that seems "religious," and most religious publishers are terrified of seeming to have been influenced by the secular world out there. But both kinds of songs have lifted our souls, so they belong together.

We've tried to be selective. Whether silly or serious, the songs we chose had to be among those that we enjoyed singing with others, that lifted our spirits and grounded the community in musical and lyrical harmony. Songs tend to stick in the heart forever. People who have lost the ability to speak can often still sing songs they learned long before. We wanted to make sure these were songs we'd want sticking in people's hearts!

We weren't able to include **all** our favorites, unfortunately. For their own reasons, some companies flatly refused our request to reprint their songs. Others required royalties so high they would have scuttled the whole project.

Some of the "old chestnuts" have a rather strong shell, somewhat resistant to change. So, while we would have preferred that all of the songs have inclusive language and imagery, they don't. Not all of the people who own the copyright on these pieces share our enthusiasm for inclusive images, so we decided to let some of the outdated images stay. The alternative was to exclude the song. Music of the community is always a mixture of this moment in our collective journey. Besides, of course, like all good songs, you'll sing them the way you want, anyway.

We recognize, too, that every group or camp or community has its own traditions. You may well have sung these songs differently in the first place, or variations in the words or the tune or the actions. Where we could, we've indicated alternatives. But if we didn't, we trust you to work it out.

Because in any community, there are a lot more singers than musicians, we've slanted this book toward singers. So we have included the melody line and the chords, but not a full music score. Sometimes we had to make difficult choices, between setting up the notes the way musicians like them, or setting up the words so that singers can read them more easily. Wherever we had to make that choice, we've leaned towards the singers. We hope that those of you who play the piano or guitar will be able to adjust to any inconvenience as a result.

We'd love to hear from you about those songs that you wish had been included. And we'd like to hear how some of these songs brought back memories for you, as they did for Kate and me.

— **Mardi Tindal**

Gathering songs

Your parents probably quoted you this helpful advice: "You never get a second chance to make a good first impression." They were right. And the maxim holds true for community building when people get together.

Every gathering is new, and what happens at the beginning—whether it's the start of a conference, a meeting, a worship session, or a campfire—the songs you sing will set the tone for your time together.

One of the marvellous things about music is its ability to pull people together emotionally and spiritually. So if that's what you want to accomplish at the start of an event, well chosen songs will go a long way towards reaching your goal.

1. The more we get together

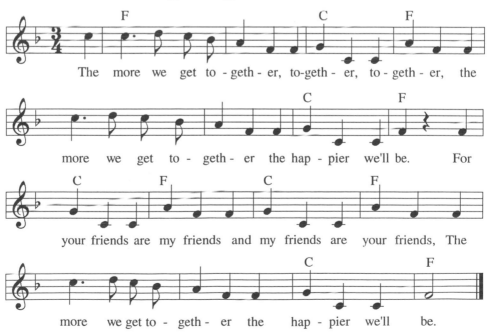

The more we get to-geth-er, to-geth-er, to-geth-er, the
more we get to-geth-er the hap-pier we'll be. For
your friends are my friends and my friends are your friends, The
more we get to-geth-er the hap-pier we'll be.

2. Come join the circle

1. Come join the cir - cle for Je - sus is call- ing, as part-ners with
2. Now say "Hel - lo" to the per - son be - side you, and wel-come them
3. O - pen the cir - cle for oth -ers are call- ing us, call-ing from

God in cre - a - tion. All join your hands now let all be in-
in - to the cir - cle. Each has a gift or a tal-ent worth
past and from fu - ture. Chal- leng-ing us with their cry for

clud - ed for this is a great cel - e - bra - tion.
shar - ing as part of their call - ing to ser - vice.
jus - tice as part of this glo - bal com - mu - ni - ty.

Look a - round and see who's here, look at all the fa -

ces. This is the cir - cle of vi - sions and dreams of

peo - ple from all times and pla - ces.

Words and music: Gordon Webber

3. One more step

1. One more step a-long the world I go. One more step a-long the
2. Round the cor-ner of the world I turn. More and more a-bout the
3. As I tra-vel through the bad and good, Keep me tra-vel-ling the

world I go. From the old things to the new
world I learn. All the new things that I see
way I should. Where I see no way to go

Keep me tra - vel - ling a - long with you. And it's from the old I
You'll be look - ing at a - long with me.
You'll be tell - ing me the way, I know.

tra - vel to the new. Keep me tra - vel - ling a - long with you.

4. Give me courage when the world is rough.
   Keep me loving though the world is tough.
   Leap and sing in all I do.
   Keep me travelling along with you.

5. You are older than the world can be.
   You are younger than the life in me.
   Ever old and ever new.
   Keep me travelling along with you.

Words and music: Sydney Carter (Original title: "Travelling with God")
Tune name: "Southcote"

4. Something to sing about

1. I have walked 'cross the sand on the Grand Banks of New-found-land,
2. I have wel - comed the dawn from the fields of Sas - kat - che - wan,
3. I have heard the wild wind sing the pla - ces that I have been,
4. I have wan - dered my way to the wild - wood of Hud-son Bay,

Lazed on the ridge of the Mi - ra - mi - chi. Seen the
Fol - lowed the sun to the Van - cou - ver shore. Watched it
Bay Bulls and Red Deer and Strait of Belle Isle. Names like
Trea - ted my toes to Que - bec's mor - ning dew. Where the

waves tear and roar at the stone coast of Lab - ra - dor,
climb shi - ny new up the snow peaks of Car - i - boo,
Grand' mère and Sil - ver - throne, Moose Jaw and Mar - row - bone,
sweet sum-mer breeze kissed the leaves of the ma - ple trees,

Watched them roll back to the great north - ern sea.
Up to the clouds where the wild Roc - kies soar.
Trails of the pi - o - neer, named with a smile.
Shar - ing this song that I'm sing - ing to you.

5. Yes, there's something to sing about, tune up a string about,
   Call out in chorus or quietly hum
   Of a land that's still young with a ballad that's still unsung
   Telling the promise of great things to come.

Words and music: Oscar Brand

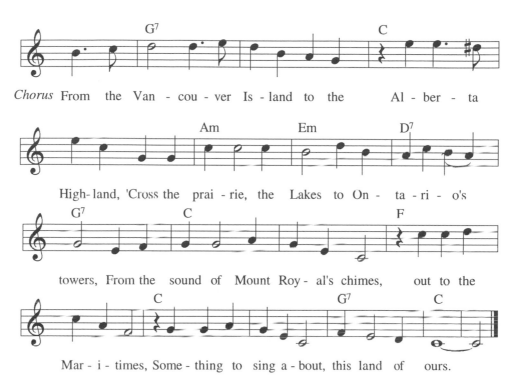

Chorus From the Van - cou - ver Is - land to the Al - ber - ta

High- land, 'Cross the prai - rie, the Lakes to On - ta - ri - o's

towers, From the sound of Mount Roy - al's chimes, out to the

Mar - i - times, Some - thing to sing a - bout, this land of ours.

Oscar Brand was born in Winnipeg. He wrote this song for a television special in 1963.

5. You gotta sing when the Spirit says "Sing"

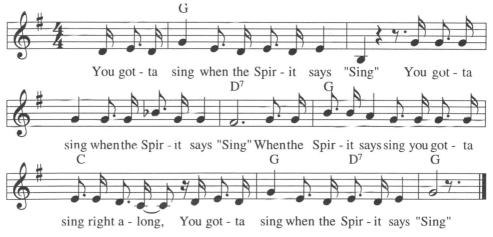

You got - ta sing when the Spir - it says "Sing" You got - ta

sing when the Spir - it says "Sing" When the Spir - it says sing you got - ta

sing right a - long, You got - ta sing when the Spir - it says "Sing"

For additional verses, substitute "shout", "pray", "laugh", "preach", or any other suitable word for "sing". Usually, the final verse reverts to "sing". Some traditions sing "I'm gonna..." instead of "You gotta..."

6. Thank you

1. Thank you for giv - ing me the morn - ing,
2. Thank you for all my friends and oth - ers,
3. Thank you, I have my oc - cu - pa - tion,
4. Thank you for ma - ny lit - tle sor - rows,

Thank you for ev - ery day that's new,
Thank you for ev - ery - one who lives,
Thank you for ev - ery pleas - ure small,
Thank you for ev - ery kind - ly word,

Thank you that I can know my wor - ries
Thank you for ev - en great - est en - em-
Thank you for mu - sic, light and glad - ness,
Thank you that ev - ery - where your guid - ance

can be cast on you.
ies I can for - give.
Thank you for them all.
reach - es ev - ery land.

Words and music: M. G. Schneider
Translation: Walter van der Haas, Peter-Paul van Lelyveld and others
Printed with the permission of Bosworth and Co. Ltd., London.

5. Thank you, I see your word has meaning,
   Thank you, I know your spirit here,
   Thank you, because you love all people,
   Those both far and near.

6. Thank you, O Lord you spoke unto us,
   Thank you, that for our words you care,
   Thank you, O Lord you came among us,
   Bread and wine to share.

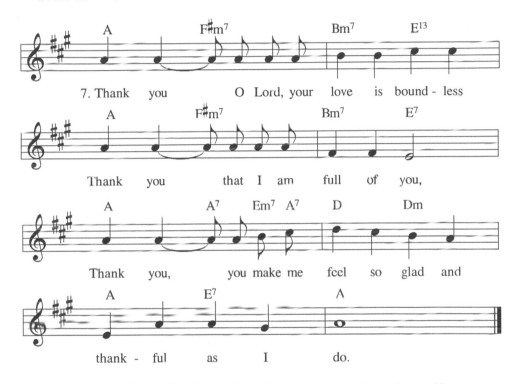

7. Thank you O Lord, your love is bound - less

Thank you that I am full of you,

Thank you, you make me feel so glad and

thank - ful as I do.

This piece may begin in the key of E and be raised a semitone for each verse, ending in the key of B flat. Or the key change may be reserved for the final verse only, as shown above. Or the key change may be ignored entirely.

7. This land is your land

Canadian chorus This land is your land, this land is my land,
American chorus This land is your land, this land is my land,

from Bon - a - vis - ta to Van - cou - ver
from Cal - i - forn - ia to the New York

Is - land, from the Arc - tic O - cean to the Great Lakes'
Is - land, from the red-wood for - est to the Gulf Stream

wa - ters, this land was made for you and me.
wa - ters, this land was made for you and me.

1. As I was walking that ribbon of highway
   I saw above me that endless skyway,
   I saw below me that golden valley
   This land was made for you and me.

2. I've roamed and rambled, and I followed my footsteps
   To the sparkling sands of the diamond deserts
   And all around me, a voice was sounding
   This land was made for you and me.

3. When the sun came shining, and I was strolling,
   And the wheat fields waving, and the dust clouds rolling,
   As the fog was lifting, a voice was chanting,
   This land was made for you and me.

Words and music: Woody Guthrie

8. Oh be joyful, oh be jubilant

Oh be joy - ful Oh be ju - bi - lant! Put your sor - row far a - way.

Come re - joice and sing to - geth - er this hap - py day.

Oh be joy - ful, Oh be joy - ful! Oh be

joy - ful, put your sor - row a - way. Oh be joy-

ful, Oh be joy - ful on this day.

This song is usually sung as three distinct parts, but can be sung as a round.

Words and music: OH BE JOYFUL, from GAUDEAMUS HODIE, by Natalie Sleeth.

Copyright © 1972 by Carl Fischer, Inc., New York. This arrangement copyright © 1994 by Carl Fischer, Inc., New York. Used by permission.

9. Ha-la-la-la (Grab another hand)

1. Grab an-oth-er hand, grab a hand next to ya, Grab an-oth-er hand and
2. Shake an-oth-er hand, shake a hand next to ya, Shake an-oth-er hand and
3. Clap an-oth-er hand, clap a hand next to ya, Clap an-oth-er hand and
4. Raise an-oth-er hand, raise a hand next to ya, Raise an-oth-er hand and

sing this song. Grab an-oth-er hand, grab a hand next to ya, Grab
sing this song. Shake an-oth-er hand, shake a hand next to ya, Shake
sing this song. Clap an-oth-er hand, clap a hand next to ya, Clap
sing this song. Raise an-oth-er hand, raise a hand next to ya, Raise

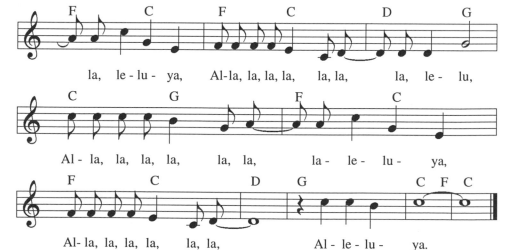

an-oth-er hand and sing, sing this song, Al-la, la, la, la, la,
an-oth-er hand and sing, sing this song,
an-oth-er hand and sing, sing this song,
an-oth-er hand and sing, sing this song,

la, le-lu - ya, Al-la, la, la, la, la, la, la, le - lu,

Al - la, la, la, la, la, la, la - le - lu - ya,

Al- la, la, la, la, la, la, Al - le - lu - ya.

Almost any action within reason can be incorporated into this song: "Scratch another back..." "Pat another head..." "Hug another friend..."

Words and music: David Graham

10. Morning has broken

1.4. Morn-ing has brok - en like the first morn - ing,
2. Sweet the rain's new fall, sun - lit from heav - en,
3. Mine is the sun - light, Mine is the morn - ing,

Black-bird has spo - ken like the first bird.
Like the first dew - fall on the first grass.
Born of the one light E - den saw play.

Praise for the sing - ing, Praise for the morn - ing,
Praise for the sweet - ness of the wet gar - den,
Praise with e - la - tion, Praise ev - 'ry morn - ing,

Praise for them, spring - ing fresh from the word.
Sprung in com - plete - ness where God's feet pass.
God's re - cre - a - tion of the new day.

For an evening version of this song, see 129, "Evening is here now."

Words: Eleanor Farjeon Music: Gaelic melody
Words used by permission of David Higham Associates.

11. The circle

1. Feel it get-tin' near-er, my lit-tle sis-ster Feel it get-tin' clear-er,

my sweet broth-er. I can hear the whis-per of my dear fa - ther.

The cir-cle keeps grow - in' strong.

2. Wel - come stran-gers drawn to the fi - re. There is no dan-ger
3. If you hear the mu - sic, sis-ters and broth-ers, If you care to join us

no de - sire; Far from dan-ger flames get-tin' high-er
sing to - geth - er, We can make a dif-fer-ence now and for - ev - er

Bridge

The cir - cle keeps grow - in' strong. Ce-le-brate the liv-ing,

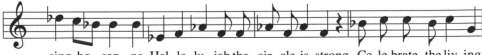

sing ho - san - na, Hal-le-lu-jah the cir-cle is strong. Ce-le-brate the liv-ing

Words and music: Colleen Peterson & Nancy Simmonds

Copyright © 1992 Nancy Simmonds, Soap Opry Music (SOCAN)
Colleen Peterson, Swofford South Music (SOCAN)

sing to the morn -ing, Hal - le -lu -jah the cir - cle is strong.

Cir - cle keeps grow - in' strong The cir-cle keeps grow - in'

strong The cir - cle keeps grow - in' strong.

This song should be performed in a "Southern Gospel" style with rhythmic stresses felt on beats two and four. Sung a cappella, performers should feel free to add improvised vocal harmonies and rhythm instruments.

12. The spirit in me

The spir - it in me greets the spir-it in you, Al - le - lu - ia.

God's in us and we're in God, Al - le - lu - ia. ia.

Repeat as often as needed, as a greeting for a gathering or as a closing. Appropriate actions vary. Some have used this song with a kind of "laying on of hands" ceremony; some use the gesture of respect used by the people of India, hands together as if in prayer in front of the chest; some use the actions shown below:

The spirit in me (point to self)
Greets the spirit in you (point to friend)
Alleluia (hands open and raised)

God's in us (grab hands)
And we're in God (cross hands over chest)
Alleluia (open hands, arms spread)

Words and music: Jim Strathdee

13. Moses

1. Mo - ses I know you're the one, the Lord said.
2. Don't get too set in your ways, the Lord said.
3. No mat - ter what you may do, the Lord said.
4. Look at the birds in the air, the Lord said.

You're going to work out my plan, the Lord said.
Each step is on - ly a phase, the Lord said.
I shall be faith - ful and true, the Lord said.
They fly un - ham - pered by care, the Lord said.

Lead all the Is - rael - ites out of sla - ve-
I'll go be - fore you and I shall be a
My love will strength - en you as you go a-
You will move ea - si - er if you're trav' - ling

ry, And I shall make them a wan - der - ing
sign To guide my trav - el - ing, wan - der - ing
long, For you're my trav - el - ing, wan - der - ing
light, For you're a wan - der - ing, vag - a - bond

race Called the Peo - ple of God. So ev - 'ry
race, You're the Peo - ple of God.
race, You're the Peo - ple of God.
race, You're the Peo - ple of God.

Words and music: Estelle White

Adapted slightly from "The People of God." Copyright © Stainer & Bell Ltd. & Mayhew
McCrimmon, Ltd. Copyright controlled in the USA by Galaxy Music Corporation, Boston, Mass.,
and by Stainer & Bell Ltd. for the rest of the world..

day - We're on our way - For we're a

trav-el-ling, wan - der-ing race. We're the Peo - ple of God.

14. Vive la compagnie

1. Come all you good peo-ple and join in the song,
2. A friend on the left and a friend on the right, Vi-ve la com - pag-
3. Now wid - er and wid - er the cir - cle ex-pands,

Suc - cess to each oth - er and pass it a - long,
nie! In love and good fel-low-ship let us u - nite, Vi - ve la com-pag-
We sing to our com-rades in far - a -way lands,

nie! Vi - ve la, vi - ve la, vi - ve l'a - mour,

Vi - ve la, vi - ve la, vi - ve l'a - mour, Vi - ve l'a - mour,

vi - ve la vie! Vi - ve la com - pag - nie!

Graces

Even in our increasingly secular world, it's still customary to have grace before community meals. And very often, when we get together, we get together over some kind of meal.

In an increasingly hectic world, too, few of us make time for the spiritual disciplines which nourish our most important relationship—the relationship with God. We rush from one activity to another, wolf down our meals, and wonder why it feels something is missing from our lives. Grace before a meal becomes a time for reconnection and recollection.

Like other songs, graces can lift the spirit and inspire us to live each moment as people of faith.

15. For health and strength

For health and strength and dai - ly food, we give you thanks, O God!

Can be sung as a round.

16. Praise God for bread

Morn - ing
Noon - time has come, the board is spread. Thanks be to
Eve - ning

God who gives us bread; Praise God for bread!

In singing this grace, choose the appropriate opening word to suit the time of day.

Attributed to A.R. Ledoux

17. Be present at our table, Lord

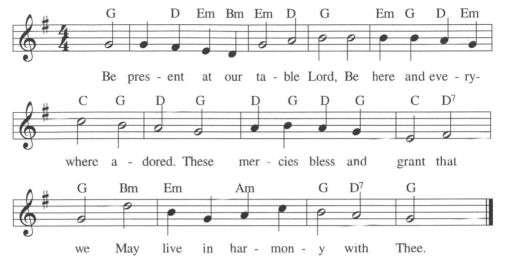

Be pres - ent at our ta - ble Lord, Be here and eve - ry-
where a - dored. These mer - cies bless and grant that
we May live in har - mon - y with Thee.

A variety of last lines are often used with this grace:
May live in fellowship with Thee.
May feast in Paradise with Thee.
May strengthened for Thy service be.
May spend our lives in serving Thee.

Words: unknown Music: Louis Bourgeois, in Genevan Psalter, 1551

18. O, give thanks

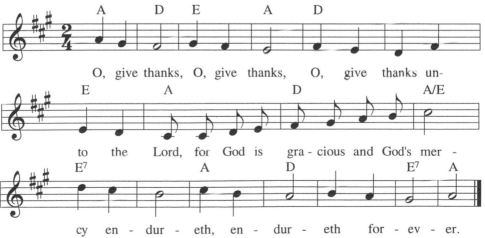

O, give thanks, O, give thanks, O, give thanks unto the Lord, for God is gra - cious and God's mer -
cy en - dur - eth, en - dur - eth for - ev - er.

19. Banquet earth grace

Cha - pa - thi, Cha - pa - thi, Pu - ri and rice! Bur-
ri - to, ta - qui - to spa - ghet - ti and spice! Dim
sum, egg foo yong, Two all - beef pat - ties, spec - ial sauce on a
bun. Hands a - cross the ta - ble, hands a - cross the
sea, Sha - ring in the ban - quet of the earth! Thanks!

Notes are given here only to show duration. Typically, this grace is chanted or shouted.

Words and music: Linnea Good

Copyright © 1989 Borealis Music, 951 Semlin Drive, Vancouver, BC, V5L 4J7.

20. Hark to the chimes

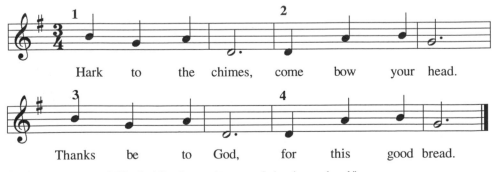

Hark to the chimes, come bow your head.
Thanks be to God, for this good bread.

Can be sung as a round. The final line is sometimes sung "who gives us bread."

21. Let us break bread

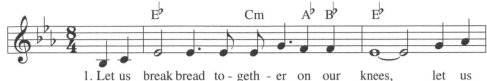

1. Let us   break bread to - geth - er on   our   knees,   let   us
2. Let us   drink wine to - geth - er on   our   knees,   let   us
3. Let us   praise God to - geth - er on   our   knees,   let   us

break bread to- geth-er on our knees. When I fall down on   my
drink wine to- geth-er on our knees.
praise God to geth-er on our knees.

knees with my face to the ris-ing sun, Oh,   Lord have mer-cy on   me.

This song can be used as a grace, but is most commonly sung as part of a communion service.

22. God Creator

God Cre - a - tor,   God Cre - a - tor,   we give thanks, we give thanks,

for   our man - y   bless - ings,   for   our   man - y   bless - ings,

We   thank   you,   We   thank   you.

23. Hot meal grace

Thank you, God for the rain and land.

Thank you, God for our work - ing hands.

Thank you for food for bod - y and soul, and

if we keep thank - ing it's gon - na get cold! It's

gon - na get col - der and we're gon - na get old-

er, so we'd bet - ter get bol - der and eat!

Words and music: Linnea Good

24. God has created a new day

God has cre - a - ted a new day, sil - ver and green and gold;

Live that the sun - set may find us wor - thy these gifts to hold.

Words and music: attributed to Marie Gaudette

25. Thanks

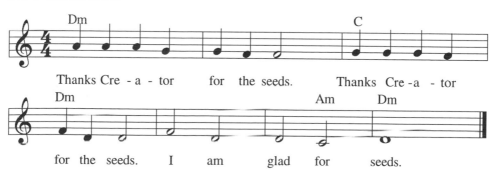

Thanks Cre - a - tor for the seeds. Thanks Cre - a - tor

for the seeds. I am glad for seeds.

This chant can go on and on as singers suggest things they are grateful for.
Options: you may beat your hands on your knees as you sing; you may substitute "Thank you, thank you" for "Thanks, Creator."

Selection taken from "All My Relations," compiled by Catherine Verrall in consultation with Lenore Keeshig-Tobias, copyright © 1988, published by the Canadian Alliance in Solidarity with the Native Peoples, P.O. Box 574, Stn. P, Toronto, ON M5S 2T1, (416) 972-1573.

26. Praise God from whom all blessings flow

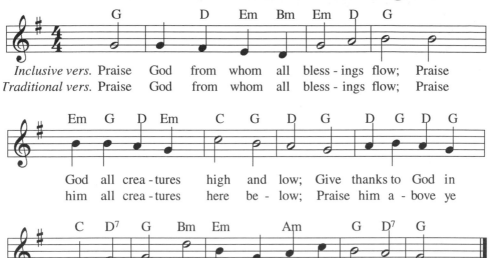

Inclusive vers. Praise God from whom all bless - ings flow; Praise
Traditional vers. Praise God from whom all bless - ings flow; Praise

God all crea - tures high and low; Give thanks to God in
him all crea - tures here be - low; Praise him a - bove ye

love made known: Cre - a - tor, Word and Spir - it One.
heaven - ly host; Praise Fa - ther, Son, and Ho - ly Ghost.

Words: adapted from Thomas Ken, 1695
Music: Louis Bourgeois in Genevan Psalter, 1551

27. Thank you for this lovely day

Thank you for this love - ly day, Guide us in the right - ful way,

Bless our fam' - lies and our friends, Bless this food thy kind hand sends.

Words and music: W. R. Ledoux

Action and fun songs

For some reason, humans have a compelling desire to be silly—sometimes. We love to laugh, and laughter is always best when we can laugh at ourselves, being silly without embarrassment.

So here's a collection of songs that will have people waving their arms, moving their bodies, making funny sounds, losing their places, and generally rediscovering the child within.

28. Alouette

Chorus Ah... A-lou-et-te, gen-tille A-lou-et-te, A-lou-et-te, je t'y plu-me-rai.

Leader

1. Je t'y plu-me-rai la têt',
2. Je t'y plu-me-rai le bec,
3. Je t'y plu-me-rai le nez,

All

Je t'y plu-me-rai la têt',
Je t'y plu-me-rai le bec,
Je t'y plu-me-rai le nez,

Leader   *All*   *Leader*   *All*

Et la têt',   Et la têt',   A-lou-ett',   A-lou-ett',
Et le bec,   Et le bec,   A-lou-ett',   A-lou-ett',
Et le nez,   Et le nez,   A-lou-ett',   A-lou-ett',

4. Je t'y plumerai les yeux... Et les yeux...
5. Je t'y plumerai le cou... Et le cou...
6. Je t'y plumerai les ail's... Et les ail's...

7. Je t'y plumerai le dos... Et le dos...
8. Je t'y plumerai les patt's... Et les patt's...
9. Je t'y plumerai la queue... Et la queue...

For each verse, repeat the items of the previous verses in reverse order. That is, the final verse should conclude: "...Et la queue... Et les patt's... Et le dos... Et les ail's... Et le cou... Et les yeux... Et le nez... Et le bec... Et la tet'... Alouett'...Oh, Alouette..."

29. If you're happy and you know it

If you're hap - py and you know it, clap your hands. If you're
                                 stamp your feet.
                                 snap your fingers.
                                 slap your thighs.

hap - py and you know it clap your hands. If you're
                               stamp your feet.
                               snap your fingers.
                               slap your thighs.

hap - py and you know it then your face will sure- ly show it. If you're

hap - py and you know it, clap your hands. If you're
                               stamp your feet.
                               snap your fingers.
                               slap your thighs.

5. Say "We are!"
6. Do all five.

In the last verse, the music stops while singers carry out all five previous actions in sequence.

30. Hokey pokey

You put your right hand in, You put your right hand out. You put your

right hand in, and you shake it all a - bout, You do the ho-key po-key, you

turn your - self a - round and that's what it's all a - bout.

Coda Oh, the ho - key po - key, Oh, the ho - key po key,

Oh, the ho - key po - key, That's what it's all a - bout!

2. You put your left hand in...
3. You put your right shoulder in...
4. You put your left shoulder in...
5. You put your right foot in...
6. You put your left foot in....
7. You put your head right in...
8. You put your whole self in...

Form a large circle. As you sing, shove the appropriate part of your anatomy in or out of the circle, and shake it. For the "hokey-pokey," put one hand on your hip, the other on top of your head, and rotate. Some traditions clap for the final two bars, some clap twice after the last word. During the optional coda, everyone joins hands and rushes to the centre on the first "Oh...", outward on the second, inward again on the third, and claps twice after the final "That's what its all about!"

31. I've got the joy, joy, joy

1. I've got the joy, joy, joy, joy, -
2. I've got the love of Je - sus, love of Je - sus
3. I've got the peace that pas - ses un - der - stand - ing

down in my heart, down in my heart, down in my

heart, I've got the joy, joy, joy, joy,
   I've got the love of Je - sus, love of Je - sus
   I've got the peace that pas - ses un - der - stand - ing

down in my heart, Down in my heart to stay.

4. And there is therefore now no condemnation, down in my heart...
5. I've got the wonderful love of the blessed Redeemer
   deep down in the depths of my heart...

Words and music originally by George W. Cooke, and others

32. She'll be comin' 'round the mountain

1. She'll be com - in' 'round the moun- tain when she comes. (toot toot)
2. She'll be driv- in' six white hor- ses when she comes. (whoa back)
3. We will all go out to meet her when she comes. (Hi, there!)
4. We will kill the old red roo- ster when she comes. (Hack, hack)

She'll be com - in' 'round the moun -tain when she comes. (toot toot)
She'll be driv - in' six white hor - ses when she comes. (whoa back)
We will all go out to meet her when she comes. (Hi, there!)
We will kill the old red roo - ster when she comes. (Hack, hack

She'll be com-in' 'round the moun-tain, she'll be com -in' 'round the
She'll be driv - in' six white hor - ses, she'll be driv - in' six white
We will all go out to meet her, we will all go out to
We will kill the old red roo - ster, we will kill the old red

moun-tain, she'll be com - in' 'round the moun-tain when she comes.
hor - ses, she'll be driv - in' six white hor - ses when she comes.
meet her, we will all go out to meet her when she comes.
roo - ster, we will kill the old red roo - ster when she comes.

5. We will all eat chicken and dumplings ... (Yum yum)
6. She will have to sleep with Grandma when she comes... (Snore snore)

At the end of each verse, do all the sounds of all previous verses in reverse order. So the final verse
would conclude: "Snore, snore; yum yum; hack hack; Hi there! whoa back; toot toot!"

33. Halle, hallelujah

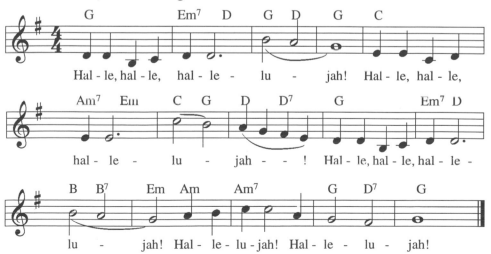

Hal - le, hal - le, hal - le - lu - jah! Hal - le, hal - le,

hal - le - lu - jah - - ! Hal - le, hal - le, hal - le -

lu - jah! Hal - le - lu -jah! Hal - le - lu - jah!

34. There's a hole in the bottom of the sea

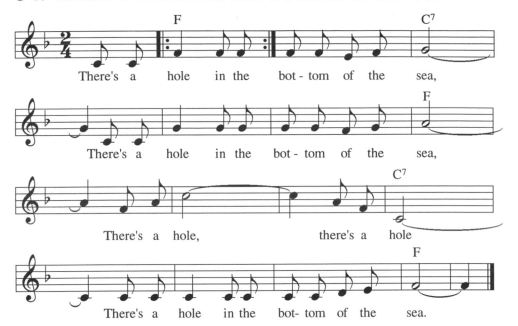

There's a hole in the bot-tom of the sea,
There's a hole in the bot-tom of the sea,
There's a hole, there's a hole
There's a hole in the bot-tom of the sea.

2. There's a log in the hole, in the bottom of the sea...
3. There's a bump on the log in the hole in the bottom of the sea...
4. There's a frog on the bump on the log in the hole in the bottom of the sea...
5. There's a wart on the frog on the bump on the log...
6. There's a hair on the wart on the frog on the bump on the log...
7. There's a flea on the hair on the wart on the frog...
8. There's a germ on the flea on the hair on the wart on the frog...

With some ingenuity and creativity, this song can be prolonged almost indefinitely. You could have a cell on the germ, or a hippopotamus, or a ...? Part of the game is not to take a breath at all during the long phrase. Once no one can sing the next verse without breaking for breath, it's time to quit.

35. Rise and shine

Chorus Rise and shine and give God the glo-ry, glo-ry,
Rise and shine and give God the glo-ry, glo-ry; Rise and shine and

give God the glo - ry, glo - ry; Chil - dren of our God.

1. God said to Noah, "There's gon-na be a floody, floody (twice)
   Get those children out of the muddy, muddy," Children of our God.

2. So Noah, he built him, he built him an arky, arky (twice)
   Made it out of gopher barky, barky, Children of our God.

3. The animals, they came in by two-zies, two-zies, two-zies (twice)
   Elephants and kangaroo-zies, roo-zies, Children of our God.

4. It rained and poured for forty day-zies, day-zies (twice)
   Nearly drove those animals crazies, crazies, Children of our God.

5. Dove went out, to take a peeky, peeky (twice)
   Dove came back with twig in beaky, beaky, Children of our God.

6. The animals they came out in three-zies, three-zies three-zies (twice)
   Must have been those birds and bee-zies, bee-zies, Children of our God.

7. This is the end of, the end of our story, story (twice)
   Everything is hunky-dory, dory, Children of our God.

A note about verse 2: according to the King James Version of the Bible, God told Noah to build the ark out of gopher-wood. (Genesis 6:14 KJV)

36. A ram sam

A ram sam sam, a ram sam sam. Gu - li
gu - li gu - li gu - li gu - li ram sam sam. A ra - fi. a
ra - fi. Gu - li gu - li gu - li gu - li gu - li ram sam sam

This spoken chant was originally supposed to have come from Morocco, but has become a campfire favorite. Among many groups, performers bounce on their seats for "ram sam sam" and stand up and extend their arms into the air for "a RA-fi." ("Guli" is pronounced "goo-lee.")

37. Singin' in the rain

To turn this into a cheerful rainy-day fun song, simply add an action each time you sing through the song. Suggestions might be: sing while skipping around in a circle, swinging your arms up and down, squatting and rising, blinking your eyes, twisting around... The more these actions can be combined, the more hilarious and exhausting the result.

Words: Arthur Freed Music: Nacio Herb Brown

38. This little light of mine

This lit-tle light of mine. I'm gon-na let it
Hide it un-der a bushel, No! I'm gon-na let it
Don't let a-ny-one whff (blow) it out, I'm gon-na let it

shine. This lit-tle light of mine.
shine. Hide it un-der a bushel, No!
shine. Don't let a-ny-one whff (blow) it out,

I'm gon-na let it shine. This lit-tle light of
I'm gon-na let it shine. Hide it un-der a
I'm gon-na let it shine. Don't let a-ny-one

mine. I'm gon-na let it shine. Let it
bushel, No! I'm gon-na let it shine.
whff (blow) it out, I'm gon-na let it shine.

shine, let it shine, let it shine.

4. Let it shine in my hometown. (3x) I'm gonna let it shine.
5. See the light spreading round the world. (3x) See all the faces shine.

Actions:
Verse 1. Hold up right forefinger to represent point of shining light.
Verse 2. Hold left hand, palm down, as cover over right forefinger; when you shout "No!" extend both hands and shake head vigorously.
Verse 3. For "whff" blow at the top of right forefinger as if blowing out a candle, but say the words "it out."

39. Six little ducks

Six lit - tle ducks that I once knew, Fat ones, skin-ny ones,
Down to the riv - er they would go, Wibble wobble, wib-ble wobble,
Home from the riv - er they would come, Wibble wobble, wib-ble wobble,

tall ones, too. But the one lit - tle duck with a feath - er on its back,
to and fro,
ho ho hum,

It led the oth - ers with a quack, quack, quack, quack, quack, quack,

quack, quack, quack! It led the oth - ers with a quack,quack, quack!

Actions:

"Six" hold up six fingers	"Too" or "to" hold up two fingers
"I" point to self	"One" hold up one finger
"Fat" spread hands out	"Feather" hand behind back
"Skinny" bring hands close together	"Led" beckon neighbor to follow
"Tall" reach for the sky	"Quack" open and close hands like duck's bill

40. Three blue pigeons

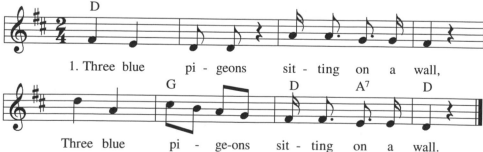

1. Three blue pi - geons sit - ting on a wall,

Three blue pi - ge-ons sit - ting on a wall.
(Spoken by one person) One of them flew away. (All, sadly) Awwwwwww.

2. Two blue pigeons sitting on a wall...
(Spoken) Another pigeon flew away. (All, more sadly) Awwwwwwww.

3. One blue pigeon sitting on a wall...
(Spoken) And the third one flew away (All) Awwwwwwwww.

4. No blue pigeons sitting on a wall...
(Spoken) One of the pigeons came back! (All) Wheeeeeeee!

5. One blue pigeon sitting on a wall....
(Spoken) And another flew back! (All) Wheeeeeee!

6. Two blue pigeons sitting on a wall....
(Spoken) And the third one came back! (All) Wheeeeeeeeee!

7. Three blue pigeons sitting on a wall....
(Spoken) There's nothing more to say!

41. Three little piggies

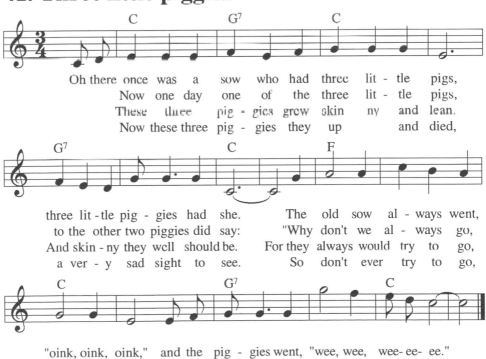

Oh there once was   a   sow   who had three   lit - tle   pigs,
Now   one   day   one   of   the three   lit - tle   pigs,
These   three   pig - gies grew skin   ny   and   lean.
Now these three pig - gies they   up   and   died,

three lit - tle pig - gies had   she.   The   old   sow   al - ways went,
to the other two piggies did say: "Why don't we   al - ways   go,
And skin - ny they well should be.   For they always would try   to   go,
a ver - y   sad sight to   see.   So   don't ever   try   to   go,

"oink, oink, oink," and the pig - gies went, "wee, wee, wee- ee- ee."
'oink, oink, oink,' It's so   chil - dish to go 'wee, wee, wee- ee- ee.'"
"oink, oink, oink," But could on - ly go "wee, wee, wee- ee- ee."
"oink, oink, oink," When you ough - ta go "wee, wee, wee- ee- ee."

The concluding bars should sound like a declining squeal, but may be sung an octave lower.

42. Old MacDonald had a farm

Old Mac-Don-ald   had   a   farm, E, I, E, I,   O!

On this farm he   had some chicks   E, I, E, I, O! with a
On this farm he   had some ducks   E, I, E, I, O! with a
On this farm he   had a   tur-key   E, I, E, I, O! with a
On this farm he   had a   pig   E, I, E, I, O! with an

*chick   chick   here and a   chick   chick   there;
quack   quack   here and a   quack   quack   there;
gob - ble gob - ble   here and a   gob - ble gob - ble   there;
oink   oink   here and an   oink   oink   there;

here a chick,   there a chick,   Ev - 'ry-where a chick   chick.
here a quack,   there a quack,   Ev - 'ry-where a quack   quack.
here a gob-ble, there a gob-ble, Ev - 'ry-where a gob-ble gob-ble.
here an oink,   there an oink,   Ev - 'ry-where an oink   oink.

Singers may add as many animals and animal sounds as they can think of. Each verse repeats the last two lines of all the previous verses, working backwards, between the marks * and **. The song finally ends by repeating the first line.

43. One finger, one thumb

One fin-ger, one thumb, keep mov-ing; One

fin-ger, one thumb, keep mov-ing; One fin-ger, one thumb, keep

mov-ing; We'll all be hap-py and gay!

Verse 2: One finger, one thumb, one hand, keep moving...

Continue adding body parts (more fingers, more thumbs, two hands, one arm, two arms, one leg, two legs, get up, sit down, etc.) until singers collapse from either exhaustion or hysteria.

44. Hallelu... Praise ye the Lord

Hal-le - lu! Hal-le-lu! Hal-le-lu! Hal- le-lu -jah! Praise ye the Lord! Hal-le-

lu! Hal-le-lu! Hal- le-lu! Hal-le-lu - jah! Praise ye the Lord!

Praise ye the Lord! Hal-le-lu - jah! Praise ye the Lord! Hal-le-lu -jah!

Praise ye the Lord! Hal-le-lu - jah! Praise ye the Lord!

For an action song, divide singers into two groups. Group 1 sings the "Hallelu... Hallelujah" sections; group 2 sings "Praise ye the Lord"; both groups sing final phrase together. Those who are singing stand; those who are not singing, sit.

45. Donkey riding

1. Were you ev - er in Que-bec Stow-ing tim-ber on the deck,
2. Were you ev - er off the Horn Where it's al-ways fine and warm,
3. Were you ev-er in Card-iff Bay Where the folks all shout "Hur-ray!

Where there's a king with a gold - en crown, Rid-ing on a don - key?
See - ing the Li - on and the U - ni - corn, Rid-ing on a don - key?
Here comes John with his 3 months' pay." Rid-ing on a don - key?

Chorus Hey, ho! A - way we go! Don - key rid - ing, don - key rid - ing,

Hey, ho! A - way we go! Rid - ing on a don - key.

Sailors commonly created rhymed couplets bringing in names of ports and places around the world. This song apparently originated with ships carrying lumber from Canada to ports in Britain. The "donkey" is a donkey engine used in loading cargo.

46. Jaybird

Down the road not so very far off
A jaybird died of the whooping cough.
He whooped so hard with the whooping cough
That he whooped his head and his tail right off!

This is a spoken "song"; the rhythm is evident from the words. For actions, you stand up with your arms in the air every time you say "whoop..." You can do it all together or as a round, with each new group starting in as soon as the previous group completes a line. With several groups, people will be "whooping" up and down all over the room!

47. Lying in my sleeping bag

Ly- ing in my sleep- ing bag, I could-n't fall a- sleep I
looked at my watch, and I want-ed to weep. I rolled to the
left and I rolled to the right and I heard ev-'ry sound that you can
hear at night! And this is what I heard, I

1. heard a cric- ket ch ch ch ch ch ch ch ch ch ch

2. heard a dog ar ar ar ooo ar ar ar ooo

3. heard a si- ren whee oo whee oo whee oo whee oo

4. heard a sprin- kler ch ch chch ch ch chch chch chch ppbbllbbtth

5. heard the sun rise; who oo oo oo

The final sound for the sunrise should glide upward, from low to high voice. Aside from that concluding sound, the notes are shown only to convey rhythm; this is usually done as a "rap" song.

Words and music: Linnea Good

Rounds and chants

Nothing, it seems, brings back memories like these songs. It may be that you remember your parents and aunts and uncles blending voices at a picnic. Or a group of friends gathered around a campfire. Or a church youth event... Perhaps, if you're fortunate, you still sing rounds occasionally, maybe even in your church sanctuary.

Rounds, echoes, and chants pull people together in harmony. Rounds originated as canon—a melody designed to harmonize with itself. Symbolically, they show that diversity and unity are both possible, at the same time. It's no accident that the church, social justice movements and even national independence movements have found rounds, echoes and chants powerful in binding people together in a common cause.

Some of these songs are just fun; some have kept faith alive under oppression; some have sustained spirits on picket lines and protests.

48. Kookaburra

Kook - a - bur - ra sits on the old gum tree.

Mer - ry, mer - ry king of the bush is he. Laugh, kook - a - bur - ra,
Eat - ing all the gum drops he can see. Stop, kook - a - bur - ra,
Count- ing all the mon - keys he can see. Stop, kook - a - bur - ra,

laugh, kook - a - bur - ra, Gay your life must be. Ha, ha, ha.
stop, kook - a - bur - ra, Leave some there for me. Ha, ha, ha.
stop, kook - a - bur - ra, That's not a monkey, that's me! Ha, ha, ha.

When sung as a round, usually only verse 1 is used.

Words and music: Marion Sinclair

49. Green grow the rushes, oh!

I'll sing you one oh, Green grow the rush-es oh. What is your one oh,
I'll sing you two oh,   What is your two oh?

First time only   1. One is one and all a - lone and   ev - er more shall be   so.

2. Two, two, the lil - y - white boys cloth - ed all in green,   oh.

One is one and all a - lone and   ev - er more shall be   so.

3. Three, three, the   ri - vals,   (and repeat: Two, two, the lily-white...)

Tune: verses 4, 6, 8, 10, 12   *Tune: verses 5, 7, 9, 11*

4. Four for the gospel makers
5. Five for the symbols at your door
6. Six for the six proud walkers
7. Sev'n for the seven stars in the sky
8. Eight for the April rainers

9. Nine for the nine white shiners
10. Ten for the Ten Commandments
11. 'leven for the 'leven who went to heav'n
12. Twelve for the twelve apostles

This song originated as a means of reinforcing religious teachings. Each verse is a biblical reference: Jesus is "one", the brothers James and John are the "lily-white boys," the three rivals are James, John, and Peter, etc.

50. The garbage round

One bot-tle of pop, two bot-tles of pop, three bot-tles of pop,

four bot-tles of pop, five bot-tles of pop, six bot-tles of pop,

sev - en bot-tles of pop, Pop! Don't throw your junk in my back - yard,

my back - yard, my back -yard. Don't throw your junk in

my back -yard, my back -yard's full. Fish and chips and

vi - ne - gar, vi - ne - gar, vi - ne - gar. Fish and chips and

vi - ne - gar. Pep - per, pep - per, pep - per Pop!

This round can be sung as three separate parts, with each of three groups taking the "bottle,"
"junk," and "fish-and-chips" parts. Or it can be sung as a traditional round, with each group singing
all three parts in succession. Caution: some happy campers like to use the middle "junk" portion to
drown out leaders attempting to make announcements.

51. Three blind mice

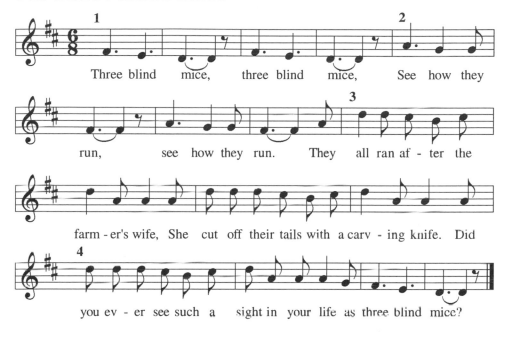

Three blind mice, three blind mice, See how they run, see how they run. They all ran af - ter the farm - er's wife, She cut off their tails with a carv - ing knife. Did you ev - er see such a sight in your life as three blind mice?

52. I love the mountains

I love the moun-tains, I love the rol-ling hills, I love the flow -ers, I love the daf-fo- dils; I love the fire - side when all the lights are low; Boom - dee - ah - da, Boom - dee - ah - da, Boom - dee - ah - da, Boom - dee - ah - da.

53. Row, row, row your boat

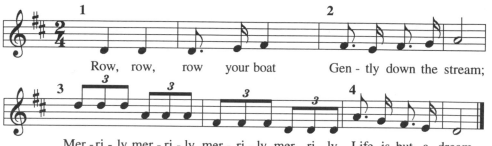

Row, row, row your boat Gen - tly down the stream;

Mer - ri - ly, mer - ri - ly, mer - ri - ly, mer - ri - ly, Life is but a dream.

54. Are you sleeping?/Frère Jacques

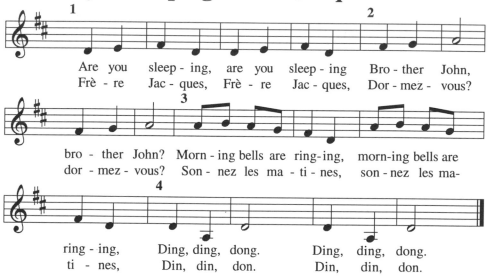

Are you sleep - ing, are you sleep - ing Bro - ther John,
Frè - re Jac - ques, Frè - re Jac - ques, Dor - mez - vous?

bro - ther John? Morn - ing bells are ring-ing, morn-ing bells are
dor - mez - vous? Son - nez les ma - ti - nes, son - nez les ma-

ring - ing, Ding, ding, dong. Ding, ding, dong.
ti - nes, Din, din, don. Din, din, don.

While "Row, row, row your boat," "Are you sleeping/Frère Jacques," and "Three blind mice" (number 51 on the previous page) are all legitimate rounds in their own right, they can also be combined into a single round with part of the group singing each song. If you also treat each individual song as a four-part round, you could have as many as 12 parts singing at once!

55. Make new friends

Make new friends but keep the old: One is sil-ver and the oth-er gold.

56. Thank you tree

Thank you tree for sing-ing your song, Breath-ing
Thank you tree for hold-ing the land, Shel-ter-
Thank you tree for be-ing a home, Bird and

with me all my life long; Thanks for stand-ing so tall and
ing us in sun and wind. Shim'-ring and danc-ing over me
in-sect, wa-ter and stone. All my re-la-tions, none is a-

strong. Tree I'm lov-ing you all my life long.
bend. Tree I'm list-en-ing, I am your friend.
lone. Tree I'll care for you all my life long.

Selection taken from "All My Relations," compiled by Catherine Verrall in consultation with Lenore Keeshig-Tobias, copyright © 1988, published by the Canadian Alliance in Solidarity with the Native Peoples, P.O. Box 574, Stn. P, Toronto, ON M5S 2T1, (416) 972-1573.

57. Hey, ho, nobody home

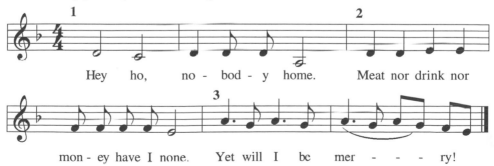

Hey ho, no-bod-y home. Meat nor drink nor

mon-ey have I none. Yet will I be mer - - - ry!

This round is supposedly the words of a gypsy or tinker, finding a house whose owners are away, with the door unlocked and the contents unguarded.

58. We all fly like eagles

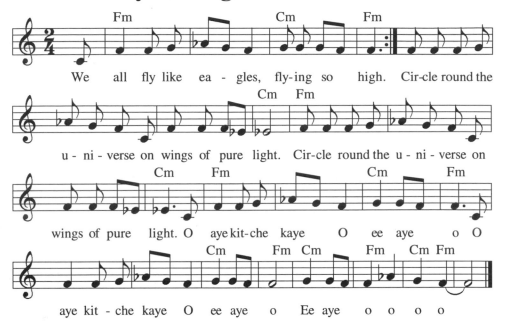

We all fly like ea - gles, fly-ing so high. Cir-cle round the u - ni - verse on wings of pure light. Cir-cle round the u - ni - verse on wings of pure light. O aye kit-che kaye O ee aye o O aye kit - che kaye O ee aye o Ee aye o o o o

Selection taken from "All My Relations," complied by Catherine Verrall in consultation with Lenore Keeshig-Tobias, copyright © 1988, published by the Canadian Alliance in Solidarity with the Native Peoples, P.O. Box 574, Stn. P, Toronto, ON M5S 2T1, (416) 972-1573.

59. Chairs to mend

Chairs to mend, old chairs to mend, Mack - er - el, fresh mack - er - el, An - y old rags, An - y old rags?

In olden days, peddlars of many kinds moved up and down streets, turning them into a kind of mobile marketplace. This round recreates the variety of cries and calls.

60. What does the Lord require?

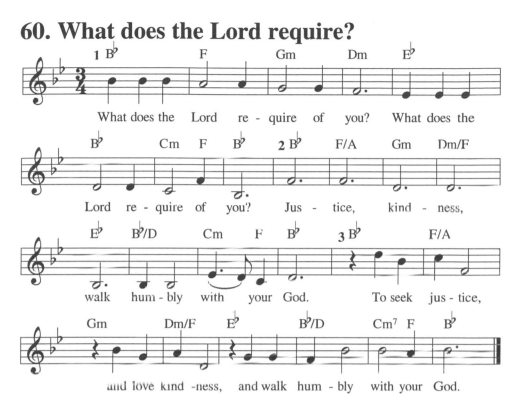

This can be sung as a regular round, but Jim Strathdee recommends having basses sing part 1, tenors and altos part 2, and sopranos part 3, repeating their own parts until it's time to end the song.

Words: Micah 6:8 Music: Jim Strathdee

Copyright © 1986 by Desert Flower Music, P.O. Box 1476, Carmichael, CA 95609.
Used by permission.

61. Oh, how lovely is the evening

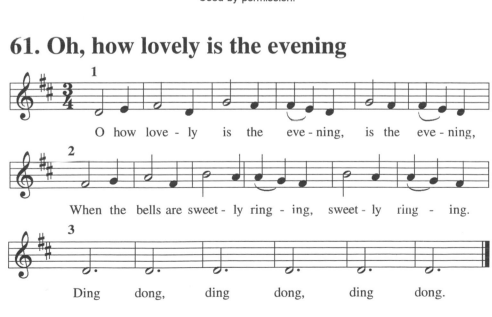

62. My paddle's keen and bright

My   pad - dle's keen and bright, Flash - ing like sil - ver;
Dip,   dip,   and swing her back, Flash - ing like sil - ver,

Fol - low   the   wild goose flight, Dip, dip, and swing.
Fol - low   the   wild goose track, Dip, dip, and swing.

This song (often also known as the "Canoe Round") may be sung as a round. It's not limited to
two groups, but each successive group comes in at the same place. Or it can be combined with
"Land of the Silver Birch," number 64, with each of two groups singing their own song.

63. Barges

1. Out   of   my win - dow   look - ing in the night,   I can
   Si - lent - ly flows   the   ri - ver to the sea, And the
3. Out   of   my win - dow   look - ing in the night,   I can
   Star - board shines green and   port is glow - ing red, You can

see   the   bar - ges' fli - cker - ing light;   2. Bar - ges,   I would
bar - ges too   go si - lent - ly.   Bar - ges, have you
see   the   bar - ges' fli - cker - ing light;   4. (same as vs. 2)
see   them fli - cker - ing far   a - head.

like   to   go with you, I would like to sail the   o - cean blue.
trea - sures in your hold? Do you fight with pi - rates   brave and bold?

In this arrangement, the melody is the lower note. When sung as a two-part round, the second
group starts verse 1 when the first group starts verse 2/chorus. Thus the two groups alternate their
melodies.

Harmony by Annette Taylor and Elizabeth Shorten

64. Land of the silver birch

1. Land of the   sil - ver birch, home   of   the bea - ver,
2. Down in the   for - est, deep   in   the low - lands

Where still the   might - y moose wan - ders   at   will,
My heart cries   out for   thee, hills of   the   north.

Blue lake and rock - y   shore, I will   re - turn once more.

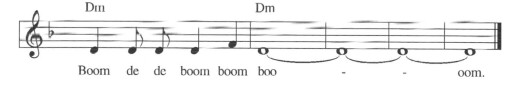

Boom   de   de   boom boom, Boom   de   de   boom boom,

Boom   de   de   boom boom boo   -   -   oom.

65. Fire's burning

Fire's burn - ing, fire's burn - ing, Draw near - er, draw near - er, In the

gloam - ing, in the gloam - ing, Come sing and be mer - ry.

66. Shri Ram, jai Ram

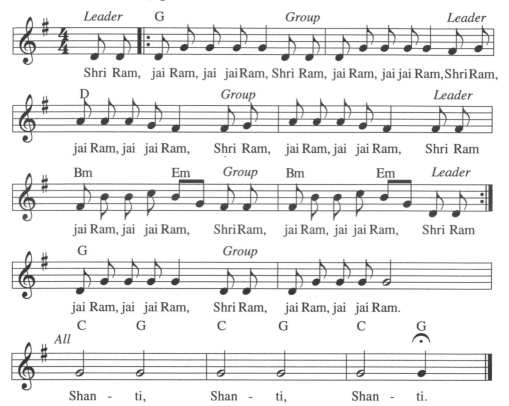

Leader   G   *Group*   *Leader*

Shri Ram,   jai Ram, jai   jai Ram, Shri Ram, jai Ram, jai jai Ram, Shri Ram,

D   *Group*   *Leader*

jai Ram, jai jai Ram,   Shri Ram,   jai Ram, jai jai Ram,   Shri Ram

Bm   Em   *Group*   Bm   Em   *Leader*

jai Ram, jai jai Ram,   Shri Ram,   jai Ram, jai jai Ram,   Shri Ram

G   *Group*

jai Ram, jai jai Ram,   Shri Ram,   jai Ram, jai jai Ram.

All   C   G   C   G   C   G

Shan - ti,   Shan - ti,   Shan - ti.

We're told that this echo chant was often used by Mahatma Gandhi at peace rallies. The text translates, very roughly, as "Holy Lord, live Lord... peace..."

67. White coral bells

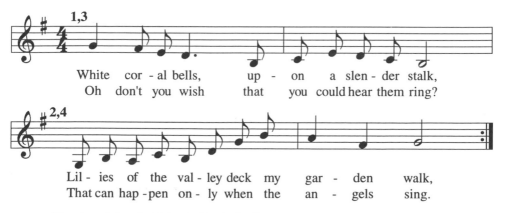

1,3

White   cor - al bells,   up - on   a slen - der stalk,
Oh   don't you wish   that   you could hear them ring?

2,4

Lil - ies   of   the   val - ley deck my   gar - den   walk,
That can hap - pen on - ly when the   an - gels   sing.

Some traditions have "when the fairies sing" in the last line.

Earth songs

Songs about the earth are not new. Most of us can remember singing "White Coral Bells" when we were younger, or singing old hymns that described rolling pastures and freshly mowed fields dotted with wheat sheaves.

Have you seen flocks of geese and ducks blanketing the sky as they migrate? Today, the wetlands that make a home for these migrating birds have all but disappeared.

A powerful sense of urgency has recently emerged in songs about the earth. DDT, acid rain, deforestation, and nuclear fallout have replaced the pastoral themes we once sang.

The earth has changed. Can we realize before it is too late, as Marie-Lynn Hammond writes in her "Temagami Round" (82) that "we and the earth are one"? Singing together strengthens the spirit that will make this awakening possible.

68. Oats peas beans and barley

Chorus Oats peas beans and bar-ley grow, oats peas beans and bar - ley grow. Do

you or I or an - y - one know how oats peas beans and bar - ley grow?

First the farm-ers plant the seeds, Stand up tall and take their ease,
Then the farm-ers wa-ter the ground, Watch the sunshine all a - round,

Stamp their feet and clap their hands and turn a -round to view the land.
Stamp their feet and clap their hands and turn a -round to view the land.

When singing this song, especially with children, it's fun to mime the actions of the verses.

69. Take off your shoes

Chorus Take, take off your shoes, you're stand-ing on my ho - ly ground.

Take, take, take off your shoes, you're stand-ing on my ho - ly

ground. Well, the earth is the Lord's and the full-ness there-of from the

wa-ters be-neath to the hea-vens a - bove, So take, take, take off your

shoes you're stand-ing on my ho - ly ground, you're

1-3. stand -ing on my ho - ly ground.

4. stand-ing on my ho- ly ground, You're stand-ing on my

ho - ly ground.

Words and music: James K. Manley

1. On the eighth day of cre-a- tion,well, the Lord looked a-round at the
2. You've heat- ed up my ri-vers with your plants and your mills, You're
3. I   dig your sci-en-ti-fic minds but use them with care, You're

pow-er plants and free- ways and the trash on the ground, Plan-
kill-ing   off   my   o - ceans with your wastes and your spills, You're
break-ing down my   o - zone lay-er   up   in the air,   Your

ta-tions grow-ing   rub-ber where the grain should be high,   You
fish ing   like there'll al-ways be   an   end- less sup - ply,   And
hyped-up farm-ing's turn-ing south-ern soil   in - to stone,   And

could-n't   see   the   sun   for   all   the smog in   the sky.   Well,
fight-ing one an - oth - er   for what's left to di - vide.   You
some are eat - ing meat while some don't e - ven get bones.   I

kids, you real - ly filled the earth and then you sub-dued   it, But there's
did - n't want ad - vice when I   first gave you do - min - ion,   But
told you to   be fruit-ful and you sure mul-ti-plied,   But the

noth - ing in   my book that says you've got to pol - lute it,   So,
may - be now it's time to get   a   sec - ond o - pin - ion, So,
rich took all   the land and nev - er learned to di - vide.   So,

70. Little boxes

Lit - tle box - es   on the hill - side, Lit - tle box - es made of
And the peo - ple in the hous - es All   go to the u-
And they all   play on the golf course And   they drink their mar-
And they all   go   in - to bus' - ness And   mar - ry and raise

tick - y tack - y, Lit - tle box - es,   lit - tle box - es, Lit - tle
ni - ver - si - ty, Where they all   get   put in box - es, And they
ti - nis dry,   And they all have pret - ty child - ren, And the
a fam - i - ly.   In   box - es   lit - tle box - es, And they

box - es   just the same. There's a green one   and a
all   come   out the same. And there's doc - tors   and there's
child - ren   go   to school. And the child - ren   go   to
all   look   just the same. There's a green one   and a

pink one And a blue one and a yel - low one, And they're
law - yers, And bus - i - ness ex - e - cu - tives. And they're
summer camp And then to the u - ni - ver - si - ty, Where they
pink one, And a blue one and a yel - low one, And they're

all made out of tick - y tack - y And they all look just the same.
all made out of tick - y tack - y And they all look just the same.
are put in   box - es   And they come out all the same.
all made out of tick - y tack - y And they all look just the same.

Words and music: Malvina Reynolds

71. Just like salt!

Je - sus said that we should be just like salt! And
if our world for - gets God, guess whose fault! Yes,
Je - sus said that we should be just like salt! And
if our world for - gets God, guess whose fault!

Last time to Coda

Salt brings out the fla - vor of food we eat
Those who fol - low Je - sus, who know God's care, are

Salt that has no salt - i - ness is thrown on the street. Oh,
those who live cre - a - tive - ly and aren't a - fraid to share, Oh,

Coda

Guess whose fault! Guess whose fault! It's mine!

Guess whose fault! It's yours! Guess whose fault! It's ours!

Words: Walter Farquharson Music: Ron Klusmeier

72. For the beauty of the earth

For the beau - ty of the earth, for the beau - ty of the skies,
For the beau - ty of each hour, of the day and of the night,
For the joy of ear and eye, for the heart and mind's de - light,
For the joy of hu - man love, bro-ther, sis-ter, par-ent, child,

For the love which from our birth ov - er and a - round us lies.
Hill and vale and tree and flower, sun and moon and stars of light.
For the my - stic har - mo - ny link - ing sense to sound and sight.
Friends on earth and friends a - bove for all gen - tle thoughts and mild.

Lord of all, to Thee we raise this our sac - ri - fice of praise.

5. For each perfect gift of thine to our world so freely given,
   Graces human and divine, flowers of earth and buds of heaven,
   Lord of all to thee we raise this our sacrifice of praise.

Words: Folliott Sandford Pierpoint, 1835-1917
Music: abridged from a chorale by Conrad Kocher, 1786-1872

73. This is my Maker's world

This is my Ma - ker's world, and to my list - 'ning ears all
This is my Ma - ker's world; the birds their ca - rols raise; the

na-ture sings, and round me rings the mu - sic of the spheres. This
mor-ning light, the li - ly white, de - clare their Ma-ker's praise. This

is my Ma-ker's world; I   rest me in the thought of
is my Ma-ker's world; God shines in all that's fair. In the

rocks and trees, of   skies and seas. God's hand the won - ders wrought.
rust - ling grass I   hear God pass; God speaks to me   ev-'ry - where.

Words: Maltbie Babcock. 1858-1901

74. Birds are singing

Birds   are sing - ing, woods are ring - ing with Thy prais - es
Wa - ters danc ing, sun - beams glanc - ing, sing Thy   glo - ry
An - gels o'er us join the cho - rus which on earth we

God a - bove; Lake   and moun-tain, field   and foun - tain,
chee - ri - ly;   Blos - soms break - ing, na - ture wa - king,
sing to Thee; Heaven is   ring - ing, earth   is   sing - ing

to Thy throne bring gifts of love.   We,   Thy child - ren
chant Thy prais - es mer - ri - ly.
Prais - es to Thee joy - ful - ly.

join the cho - rus mer - ri - ly, chee - ri - ly, glad - ly praise Thee;

Glad ho-san - nas, glad ho - san - nas, joy - ful - ly we   lift to Thee.

Words: L.F. Cole

75. The garden song

1. Inch by inch, row by row,   Gon-na make this gar-den grow,
2. Pull-in' weeds, pick-in' stones,   We are made of dreams and bones,
3. Make your rows straight and long,   Tem-per them with warmth and song,

All it takes is a rake and a hoe And a piece of fer-tile ground.
I feel a need to grow my own For the time is near at hand.
Moth-er earth will make you strong if you give her love and care.

Inch by inch, row by row Some-one bless these seeds I sow,
Grain for grain, sun and rain, Find my way thru' na-ture's chain
See that crow watch-ing hungrily From his perch on yon-der tree,

Some-one warm them from be-low Till the rain comes tum-bl-ing down.
As I tune my bod-y and my brain To the mu-sic of the land.
In my gar-den I'm as free as that fea-thered thief up there.

Words and music: David Mallett

76. God who touches earth with beauty

1. God who touch - es earth with beau - ty, make my heart a-
2. Like thy springs and run - ning wa - ters, make me crys - tal
3. Like thy dan - cing waves in sun - light, make me glad and
4. Like the arch - ing of the heav - ens lift my thoughts a-

new; with thy Spir - it re - cre - ate me pure, and strong, and true.
pure; like thy rocks of tower-ing gran-deur, make me strong and sure.
free; like the straight-ness of the pine trees let me up - right be.
bove; turn my dreams to no - ble ac - tion, mi - ni - stries of love.

5. Like the birds that soar while singing
   give my heart a song;
   may the music of thanksgiving
   echo clear and strong.

6. God who touches earth with beauty,
   make my heart anew;
   keep me ever by thy Spirit
   pure, and strong, and true.

Words: Mary Susannah Edgar, 1889-1973 Music: Henry Walford Davies, 1869-1941.
Used by permission.

77. One light, one sun

1. One light, one sun, One sun light-ing ev - 'ry - one.
2. One world, one home, One world home for ev - 'ry - one.
3. One love, one heart, One heart warm-ing ev - 'ry - one.

One world turn - ing One world turn - ing ev - 'ry - one.
One dream, one song One song heard by ev - 'ry - one.
One hope, one joy One love fill - ing ev - 'ry - one.

Coda

One light, one sun, One sun light - ing ev - 'ry - one.

One light warm - ing ev - 'ry - one.

Words and music: Raffi

78. Roots and wings

Tie me down roots and wings - - - - flow through my bran-ches the life of the earth. Teach me the an-cient songs of the soil. Let me fly, roots and wings - - - - high through the moun-tains, a - long with the clouds, fol - low my dreams as they fly. For with wat - er and bread, the sun and the air, we need roots for the ground and wings for the sky.

Words and music: Linnea Good

Dm	F	C

Spir - it of rain be my par -ent Spir - it of
Shall you find one for a lov - er? Why might you
What shall we bring as our off' - ring? With what shall we
How are you ma - king your liv - ing? Do you give

Dm	F

snow be my child. I am the oak with her
ask them to stay? Will they know the deep-push-ing
come to the day? The song of the an- cients, the
back to the earth? Have you giv -en flight to the

C	E♭	B♭

roots push-ing strong. I am the swal-low with flight in her
roots of your soul? Will theirs wrap a - round them as sea-sons grow
des-ert, the field, the song of the in- fants, the play-ground, the
dreams that you keep? Have you touched the un-der- ground streams of the

Csus⁴	C	E♭/F	F

song. I am root - ed, yet soar in the wind. Tie me
old? Will you both find your wings know the way? Tie me
wheel. In the dance of the a - ges we'll play... Tie me
deep? Come, give your im - ag - in - ings birth! Tie me

⊕ *Coda*

E♭	Cm	E♭/F	F	B♭

wings - - - - - for the sky!

79. The happy wanderer

I love to go a-wan-der-ing, A-long the moun-tain
love to wan-der by the stream That dan-ces in the
wave my hat to all I meet, And they wave back to
o-ver-head, the sky-larks wing, They nev-er rest at

track, And as I go I love to sing, My knap-sack
sun, So joy-ous-ly it calls to me, "Come! Join my
me, And black birds call so loud and sweet From ev-'ry
home, But just like me, they love to sing, As o'er the

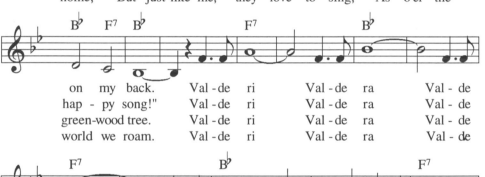

on my back. Val-de ri Val-de ra Val-de
hap-py song!" Val-de ri Val-de ra Val-de
green-wood tree. Val-de ri Val-de ra Val-de
world we roam. Val-de ri Val-de ra Val-de

ra Val-de ha ha ha ha ha ha Val-de ri,
ra Val-de ha ha ha ha ha ha Val-de ri,
ra Val-de ha ha ha ha ha ha Val-de ri,
ra Val-de ha ha ha ha ha ha Val-de ri,

Val - de ra, My knap - sack on my
Val - de ra "Come! Join my hap - py
Val - de ra, From ev - 'ry green- wood
Val - de ra, As o'er the world we

Words: Antonia Ridge   Music: Friedr. W. Möller

Printed with the permission of Bosworth & Co. Ltd., London

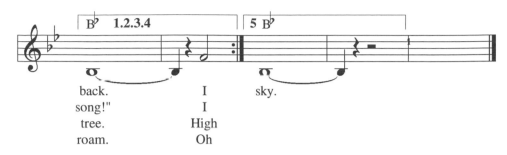

back.   I   sky.

song!"   I

tree.   High

roam.   Oh

5. Oh may I go a-wandering, Until the day I die,
     And may I always laugh and sing, Beneath God's clear blue sky!

80. All things bright and beautiful

Chorus All things bright and beau - ti - ful All crea-tures great and small.

All things wise and won der - ful, the Lord God made them all.

1. Each lit - tle flower that o - pens, each lit - tle bird that sings, God
2. The pur-ple head-ed moun-tain, the ri - ver run - ning by, The
3. The cold wind in the win - ter, the plea - sant sum - mer sun, The
4. The tall trees in the green -wood, the mea - dows where we play, The

made their glow - ing col - ours, God made their ti - ny wings.
sun - set and the mor - ning, that bright-ens up the sky.
ripe fruits in the gar - den, God made them ev' - ry one.
rush - es by the wa - ter, we ga - ther ev' - ry day.

Words: Cecil Frances Alexander 1818-1895 Music: old English melody

81. What have they done to the rain?

Just a lit - tle rain fall - ing all a - round, The
Just a lit - tle breeze out of the sky, The

grass lifts its head to the heav-en - ly sound, Just a lit - tle rain
leaves pat their hands as the breeze blows by, Just a lit - tle breeze with some

Just a lit - tle rain, What have they done to the rain?
smoke in its eye, What have they done to the rain?

Just a lit - tle boy stand - ing in the rain, The gen - tle

rain that falls for years. And the grass is gone, And the

boy dis - ap - pears, And the rain keeps fall - ing like

help - less tears, And what have they done to the rain?

This song was written during a time of concern about the dangers of radioactive fallout from nuclear testing. Malvina Reynolds avoided sweeping generalizations by writing about just one child and that child's immediate surroundings.

Words and music: Malvina Reynolds

82. Temagami Round

If we lose this for-est, if we sav-age the land,

we might as well be cut-ting off our own right hand,

for we and the earth are one,

un-der the moon, un-der the sun.

The author notes that there are no chords provided for this round, because it was written for a cappella singing. In singing it as a round, do not have additional parts enter at "forest," but at the end of the line, as indicated above. She also notes that this round, originally written for conservation concerns in northern Ontario, was also sung later by protesters at Clayoquot Sound in BC.

Words and music: Marie-Lynn Hammond

Work songs

Work may not be the first thing we think of when we gather in social groups. But work has been, and continues to be, a major element in most people's daily lives.

Work songs have often helped to make work easier, or more tolerable. Some of these songs provide snapshots of working conditions in the past. Some are protests against those working conditions.

Work songs range from the hilarious to the profound. We generally treat work songs lightly, and sing them for fun. But a few of these recognize the often harsh realities of life on the ocean, or in a mine, or as migrant labor.

83. I'se the bye

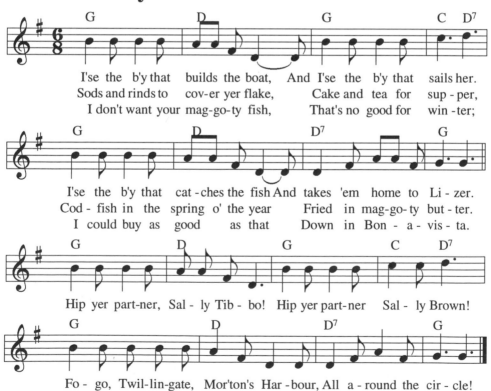

I'se the b'y that builds the boat, And I'se the b'y that sails her.
Sods and rinds to cov-er yer flake, Cake and tea for sup - per,
I don't want your mag-go-ty fish, That's no good for win -ter;

I'se the b'y that cat -ches the fish And takes 'em home to Li - zer.
Cod - fish in the spring o' the year Fried in mag-go-ty but - ter.
I could buy as good as that Down in Bon - a - vis - ta.

Hip yer part-ner, Sal - ly Tib - bo! Hip yer part-ner Sal - ly Brown!

Fo - go, Twil-lin-gate, Mor'ton's Har -bour, All a - round the cir - cle!

This song comes from Newfoundland, but is popular almost everywhere. There are a variety of additional verses, but these are the ones most commonly sung.

84. Day O

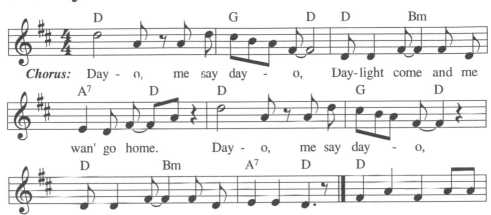

Chorus: Day - o, me say day - o, Day-light come and me

wan' go home. Day - o, me say day - o,

Day - light come and me wan' go home. 1. Work all night 'til the
2. Six foot, seven foot
4. Beauti- ful bunch of

morn - in' come, Day-light come and me wan' go home.
eight foot bunch!
ripe ba - na-na

Stack ba-na - na 'til the morn - in' come, Day-light come and me
Six foot, sev-en foot, eight foot bunch!
Hide the dead - ly black ta - ran-tula

wan'go home. 3. Come, Mis- ter Tal - ly-man, tal - ly me ba - na - na,

Day-light come and me wan' go home. Come, Mis-ter Tal- ly -man

tal - ly me ba - na - na, Day-light come and me wan' go home.

85. I've been working on the railroad

I've been work-ing on the rail-road, All the live-long day,

I've been work-ing on the rail-road, Just to pass the time a - way.

Can't you hear the whis-tle blow-ing, Rise up so ear-ly in the

morn; Can't you hear the cap-tain call-ing, "Di-nah, blow your

horn!" Din-ah, won't you blow, Di-nah, won't you blow,

Din-ah won't you blow your horn? Dina-ah won't you blow,

Din-ah won't you blow, Di-nah won't you blow your horn?

Some-one's in the kitch-en with Di-nah, Some-one's in the kitch-en I

know, Some-one's in the kitch-en with Di-nah,

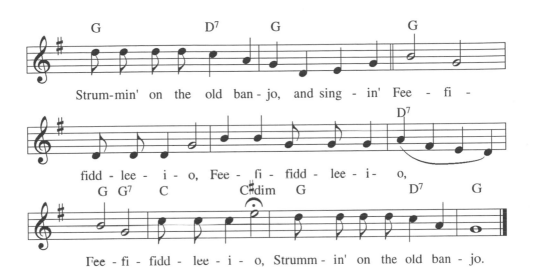

Strum-min' on the old ban-jo, and sing-in' Fee - fi -
fidd - lee - i - o, Fee - fi - fidd - lee - i - o,
Fee - fi - fidd - lee - i - o, Strumm - in' on the old ban - jo.

86. Ol' Texas

I'm	goin'	to	leave		Ol'	Tex -	as	now
They've	plowed	and	fenced		my	cat -	tle	range
The	hard,	hard	ground		will	be	my	bed
And	when	I	wake		up	from	my	dreams

They've	got	no	use		For the long - horn	cow.
And the	peo -	ple	there		are	all	so	strange.
And the	sad -	dle	seat		will	hold	my	head.
I'll	eat	my	bread		and	my	sar -	dines.

This is usually sung as an echo song. The echo is a direct repeat of the music and text printed, and starts one measure after the main verse.

87. Farewell to Nova Scotia

The sun was set - ting in the west, The
I grieve to leave my na - tive land, I
The drums they do beat and the wars do a - larm, The
I have three bro - thers and they're at rest, Their

birds were sing - ing on ev'- ry tree, All
grieve to leave my com - rades all, And my
cap - tain calls, we must o - bey. So fare-
arms are fol - ded on their breast. But a

nat - ture seemed in - clined for rest, But
par - ents whom I - hold so - dear And the
well, fare - well to Nova Sco - tia's charms, For by
poor sim - ple sail - or just like me Must be

still there was no rest for me.
bon - ny bon - ny lass that I do a - dore.
ear - ly in the mor - ning I am far, far a - way
tossed and driv - en on the deep blue sea.

Fare - well to No - va Sco - tia, the sea - bound coast! Let your

moun - tains dark and drea - ry be, For when

I am far a - way on the bri - ny o - cean tossed, Will you

e - ver heave a sigh and a wish for me?

88. Home on the range

Oh, give me a home where the buf - fa - lo roam, Where the
Where the air is so pure and the zeph - yrs so free, And the

deer and the an - te - lope play, Where sel - dom is heard a dis-
bree - zes so balm - y and light, That I would not ex - change my

cour - ag - ing word, And the skies are not cloud - y all day.
home on the range, For all of the ci - ties so bright.

Home, home on the range, Where the deer and the an - te - lope

play, Where sel - dom is heard a dis - cour - ag - ing word, And the

skies are not cloud - y all day.

Words and music: Brewster Higley, 1873

89. Plane wreck at Los Gatos (Deportee)

1. The crops are all in and the peach - es are rot - ting.
2. My fa - ther's own fa - ther, he wad - ed that ri - ver,
3. Some of us are il - leg - al, and some are not wan- ted,
4. We died in your hills, we died in your des - erts,

The or - ang - es piled in their cre - o - sote dumps.
They took all the mon - ey he made in his life;
Our work con -tract's out and we have to move on;
We died in your val - leys and died on your plains,

You're fly - ing them back to the Mex - i - can bor - der, to
My bro - thers and sis - ters come work - ing the fruit trees, and
Six hun -dred miles to that Mex - i - can bor - der, They
We died 'neath your trees and we died in your bush - es, both

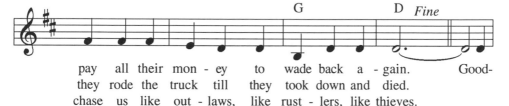

pay all their mon - ey to wade back a - gain. Good-
they rode the truck till they took down and died.
chase us like out - laws, like rust - lers, like thieves.
sides of the ri - ver, we died just the same.

5. The sky plane caught fire over Los Gatos Canyon,
   A fireball of lightning, and shook all our hills.
   Who are all these friends, all scattered like dry leaves?
   The radio says they are just deportees.

6. Is this the best way we can grow our big orchards?
   Is this the best way we can grow our good fruit?
   To fall like dry leaves to rot on my topsoil,
   And be called by no name except deportees?

Words: Woody Guthrie Music: Martin Hoffman

bye to my Juan, good-bye, Ro-sa - li-ta, a - dios, mis a - mi-gos, Je -

sus y Ma - ri - a. You won't have your names when you ride the big

air - plane, and all they will call you will be "de - por - tees."

90. Michael, row the boat ashore

Mi-chael row the boat a - shore, al - le - lu - ia! Mi-chael
Jor-dan's ri-ver is deep and wide, al - le - lu - ia! Milk and
Jor-dan's ri-ver is chil - ly and cold, al - le - lu - ia! Chills the
Sis - ter help to trim the sail, al - le - lu - ia! Sis - ter

row the boat a - shore al - le - lu - ia!
ho - ney on the oth - er side, al - le - lu - ia!
bo - dy but not the soul, al - le - lu - ia!
help to trim the sail, al - le - lu - ia!

According to Pete Seeger, this song originated among boat crews from plantations on the
Georgia Islands off the Atlantic Coast rowing their goods and produce to the mainland for sale.
The music of black slaves in the southern states often used the River Jordan as a symbol for death;
the "other side" was life beyond death.

91. Working man

Chorus It's a work-ing man I am, and I've been down un-der ground. And I swear to God if I ev-er see the sun,

Or for an-y length of time I can hold it in my mind

I nev-er a-gain will go down un-der ground.

Verse: 1. At the age of six-teen years, oh he quar-rels with his peers
2. At the age of six-ty-four, oh he'll greet you at the door

who vowed they'd nev-er see an-oth-er one.
and he'll gent - ly lead you by the arm.

In the dark re-cess of the mind where you age be-fore your
Through the dark re-cess of the mind oh he'll take you back in

Words and music: Rita MacNeil

1988, 1992 Paddy's Head Music, a division of Balmur Ltd.
(Used by permission of Warner/IChappell Music Canada Ltd.)

time, And the coal dust lies heav-y on your lungs.
time, And he'll tell you of the hard-ships that were had.

92. Clementine

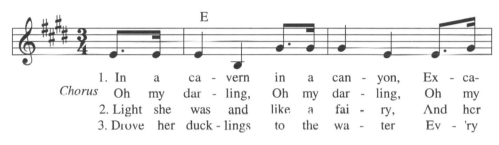

1. In a ca-vern in a can-yon, Ex-ca-
Chorus Oh my dar-ling, Oh my dar-ling, Oh my
2. Light she was and like a fai-ry, And her
3. Drove her duck-lings to the wa-ter Ev-'ry

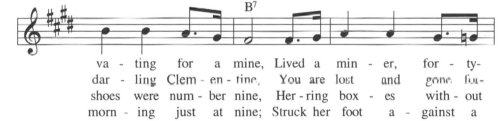

va-ting for a mine, Lived a min-er, for-ty-
dar-ling Clem-en-tine, You are lost and gone for-
shoes were num-ber nine, Her-ring box-es with-out
morn-ing just at nine; Struck her foot a-gainst a

nin-er, And his daugh-ter, Clem-en-tine.
e-ver, Dread-ful sor-ry, Clem-en-tine.
top-ses San-dals were for Clem-en-tine.
splin-ter, Fell in-to the foam-ing brine.

This song originated in the California Gold Rush of 1849, whose miners were commonly known as "forty-niners." Verse 5 below is optional!

4. Ruby lips above the water, blowing bubbles, soft and fine,
   Alas for me, I was no swimmer, so I lost my Clementine.

5. And the moral of this story is to be a Boy Scout/Girl Guide fine,
   Artificial respiration would have saved my Clementine.

93. The housewife's lament

One day I was walk-ing, I heard a com-
There's too much of wor-ri-ment goes to a
In March it is mud, it is slush in De-
There are worms on the cher-ries and slugs on the

plain-ing, and saw an old wo-man the pic-ture of gloom, She
bon-net, There's too much of iron-ing goes in-to a shirt. There's
cem-ber, The mid-sum-mer bree-zes are load-ed with dust. In
ros-es, And ants in the su-gar and mice in the pies. The

gazed at the mud on her door-step ('twas rain-ing) and
no-thing that pays for the time you waste on it, There's
fall the leaves lit-ter, in mud-dy Sep-tem-ber The
rub-bish of spi-ders no mor-tal sup-pos-es And

this was her song as she wield-ed her broom, Oh,
no-thing that lasts us but trou-ble and dirt.
wall-pa-per rots and the can-dle-sticks rust.
rav-ag-ing roach-es and dam-ag-ing flies.

Chorus

life is a toil, and love is a trou-ble, beau-ty will

fade and rich-es will flee, Plea-sures they dwin-dle and

pri-ces they dou-ble and noth-ing is   as   I would wish it to be.

5. It's sweeping at six and it's dusting at seven,
   It's victuals at eight and it's dishes at nine.
   It's potting and panning from ten to eleven,
   We scarce break our fast till we plan how to dine. (Chorus)

6. With grease and with grime, from corner to center,
   Forever at war and forever alert,
   No rest for a day lest the enemy enter,
   I spend my whole life in a struggle with dirt. (Chorus)

7. Last night in my dreams I was stationed forever
   On a far little rock in the midst of the sea.
   My one chance of life was a ceaseless endeavor
   To sweep off the waves as they swept over me. (Chorus)

8. Alas! 'Twas no dream; ahead I behold it,
   I see I am helpless my fate to avert.
   She lay down her broom, her apron she folded,
   She lay down and died and was buried in dirt. (Chorus)

This was written as a protest song out of the real experience of women in the not-too-distant past.
The song apparently originated during the Civil War years in the USA; the first known version was
copied from a diary of Mrs. Sara A. Price of Ottawa, Illinois.

94. John Henry

1. When John Hen - ry was a lit - tle ba - by, a -
2. Well the cap - tain said to John Hen - ry "Gon - na
3. John Hen - ry said to his cap - tain "Lord, a
4. John Hen - ry, he drove fif - teen feet, The

sit - ting on his pop - pa's knee, He picked up a ham-mer and a
bring that steam drill 'round. Gon-na bring that steam drill
man ain't nothin' but a man, And be - fore I'll let your
steam drill only made nine; But he ham-mered so hard that he

lit - tle piece of steel, and he said, "Ham-mer's gon - na be the death of
out on the job Gon - na whup that steel on
steam drill beat me down, I'll die with a ham -mer in my
broke his poor heart And he laid down his ham - mer and he

me, Lord, Lord" "Ham- mer's gon - na be the death of me."
down, Lord, Lord, Gon - na whup that steel on down."
hand, Lord, Lord, I'll die with a ham - mer in my hand."
died, Lord, Lord, He laid down his ham - mer and he died.

5. They took John Henry to the graveyard, And they buried him in the sand.
   And every locomotive comes a-roar-in' by, says,
   "There lies a steel-drivin' man, Lord, Lord, There lies a steel-drivin' man."

Like "The Housewife's Lament," this was originally a protest song, in this case challenging the impact
of industrialization.

95. Jack was every inch a sailor

Now, 'twas twen-ty-five or thir- ty years since Jack first saw the light, He
When   Jack grew up to be a man, he went to Lab -ra - dor; He
The   whale went off for Baf-fin Bay 'bout nine-ty knots an hour, And

came in - to this world of woe one dark and storm-y night, He was
fished in In - dian Har-bour where his fa - ther fished be- fore; On
ev - 'ry time he'd blow a spray, he'd send it in a shower." Oh

born on board his fa- ther's ship as she was ly- ing to 'Bout
his re -turn -ing in the fog, he met a hea - vy gale. And
now," says Jack un - to him-self, "I must see what he's a- bout." He

twen - ty five or thir - ty miles south - east of Bac - al hao,
Jack was swept in - to the sea and swal-lowed by a whale.
caught the whale all by the tail and turned him in - side out.

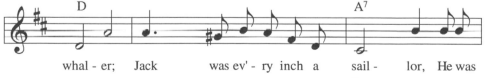

Jack was ev'- ry inch a sail -lor, Five and twen - ty years a

whal - er; Jack was ev' - ry inch a sail - lor, He was

born up - on the bright blue sea.

In the sailing dialect from which this song originated, "Bacalhao" is pronounced "back-a-loo." This song is an adaptation of the biblical Jonah story.

Traditional songs

Before the beginning of histories, people sang. Down through recorded history, people have created songs. Some have lasted no longer than the event for which they were written; others have become part of our folklore, part of the culture that surrounds us and makes us what we are.

Some songs of relatively recent origin are joining this body of folklore. Everyone knows them; everyone can sing along.

A considerable number of these traditional songs originated among people suffering oppression of various kinds, and many of the newer songs were written in support of those who were suffering or marginalized. These songs become part of our musical heritage because they transcend their original context and speak to our universal experience.

96. You are my sunshine

You are my sun-shine, my on-ly sun-shine, You make me
The oth-er night dear, as I lay sleep-ing, I dreamed I

hap-py, when skies are grey. You'll nev-er know dear,
held you by my side. But when I woke dear,

how much I love you. Please don't take my sun-shine a-way.
I was mis-tak-en, And I hung my head and cried.

This song originated during wartime, when brides often found themselves alone because their new husbands were overseas in battle. Hence the line, "I dreamed I held you... But I was mistaken..." and ends with a plea to the war itself, "Please don't take my sunshine away."

Words and music: Jimmy Davis and Charles Mitchell

97. We shall overcome

We shall o - ver - come, We shall o - ver - come,
We'll walk hand in hand, We'll walk hand in hand,
We are not a - fraid, We are not a - fraid,

We shall o - ver - come some day. Oh,
We'll walk hand in hand some day.
We are not a - fraid to - day.

deep in my heart I do be - lieve that

we shall o - ver - come some day.

This is one of those songs that has thoroughly transcended its origins. It originated during the days of slavery in the southern USA, a single verse of a hymn that began "We will overcome." It was picked up in union halls; it became a theme song of the civil rights movement of the 1960s; white youth used it during Vietnam protests; most recently, it was a rallying cry in Czechoslovakia and Hungary as those nations rejected Communism and returned to democracy.

A variety of other verses are possible, such as "The truth shall make us free..." Singers commonly make up their own verses, to suit their own situation.

Musical and Lyrical Adaptation by Zilphia Horton, Frank Hamilton, Guy Carawan and Pete Seeger. Inspired by African American Gospel Singing, members of the Food and Tobacco Workers Union, Charleston, SC, and the southern Civil Rights Movement.

98. If I had a hammer

If   I   had a   ham-mer   I'd ham-mer in the
If   I   had a   bell   I'd ring it in the
If   I   had a   song   I'd sing it in the
Well I've got a   ham-mer   And I've   got a

morn - ing,   I'd ham - mer   in   the   eve - ning,
morn - ing   I'd ring   it   in   the   eve - ning
morn - ing   I'd sing   it   in   the   eve - ning,
bell,   And I've   got a   song to sing

all   o - ver this   land,   I'd   ham - mer out
all   o - ver this   land.   I'd   ring   out
all   o - ver this   land.   I'd   sing   out
all   o - ver this   land.   It's the ham - mer of

dan - ger,   I'd   ham-mer out   a   warn - ing,
dan - ger,   I'd   ring   out   a   warn - ing,
dan - ger,   I'd   sing   out   a   warn - ing,
jus - tice,   it's   the bell of   free - dom,

I'd   ham - mer out   love be - tween   my
I'd   ring   out   love be - tween   my
I'd   sing   out   love be - tween   my
it's a song a - bout   love be - tween   my

Words and music: Lee Hays and Pete Seeger

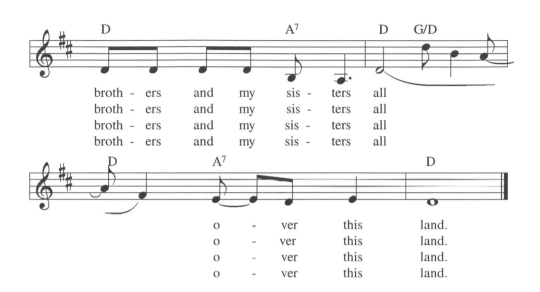

broth - ers and my sis - ters all
broth - ers and my sis - ters all
broth - ers and my sis - ters all
broth - ers and my sis - ters all

o - ver this land.
o - ver this land.
o - ver this land.
o - ver this land.

99. Peace like a river

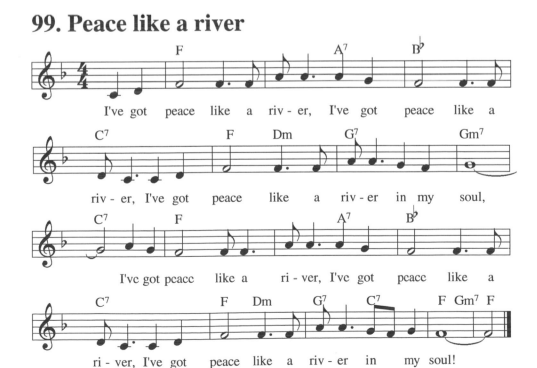

I've got peace like a riv - er, I've got peace like a

riv - er, I've got peace like a riv - er in my soul,

I've got peace like a ri - ver, I've got peace like a

ri - ver, I've got peace like a riv - er in my soul!

100. Donna donna

On a wag - on bound for mar - ket, There's a calf with a
"Stop com - plain - ing," said the far - mer, "Who told you a
Calves are ea - si - ly bound and slaugh -tered, ne - ver know -ing the

mourn - ful eye, High a - bove him there's a swal - low
calf to be? Why don't you have wings to fly with
rea - son why, But who - ev - er trea - sures free - dom,

wing-ing swift- ly through the sky. How the winds are
like the swal-low so proud and free?"
like the swal-low has learned to fly.

laugh - ing, They laugh with all their might, Laugh and laugh the

whole day through, and half the sum-mer's night. Don - na, don -na don - na,

don - na. Don - na, don-na, don - na, don. Don -na,don-na,don - na

don - na. Don - na, don - na, don - na, don.

Before it was ever translated and popularized in North America, this song was a favorite in Jewish musical theatre.

Words and music: Sholom Secunda

101. Sarah's circle

We are danc - ing Sar - ah's cir - cle, We are
We will all do our own nam - ing, We will
Here we seek and find our his - t'ry, Here we
Ev - 'ry round a gen - er - a - tion, Ev - 'ry

danc - ing Sar - ah's cir - cle, We are danc - ing
all do our own nam - ing, We will all do
seek and find our his - t'ry, Here we seek and
round a gen - er - a - tion, Ev - 'ry round a

Sar - ah's cir - cle, Sis - ters, broth - ers, all.
our own nam - ing, Sis - ters, broth - ers, all.
find our his - t'ry, Sis - ters, broth - ers, all.
gen - er - a - tion, Sis - ters, broth - ers, all.

5. Birth to death and death to birth now... (3x) Sisters, brothers, all.
6. On and on the circle's moving... (3x) Sisters, brothers, all

Words: Carole Ann Etzler   Music: "Jacob's Ladder"
Copyright © 1975 Carole A. Etzler

102. Jacob's ladder

1. We are climbing Jacob's ladder... (3x) Brothers, sisters, all.
2. Every rung goes higher, higher... (3x) Brothers, sisters, all.
3. Sinner, do you love my Jesus?... (3x) Brothers, sisters, all.
4. If you love Him, why not serve Him?... (3x) Brothers, sisters, all.

"Sarah's circle" was written as an alternative to the traditional "Jacob's ladder." The imagery of the
ladder implies climbing to the top; it reinforces the competitive streak in our society. The image of
the circle (which can be danced while being sung) emphasizes mutuality, cooperation, and
community.

103. Swing low, sweet chariot

Chorus Swing low, sweet char - i - ot, Com - in' for to car - ry me home!

Swing low, sweet char - i - ot, Com - in' for to car - ry me home.

1. I looked o - ver Jor - dan, and what did I see?
2. If you get there be - fore I do.
3. I'm some - times up and some - times down.

Com - in' for to car - ry me home! A band of an - gels
Com - in' for to car - ry me home! Just tell my friends that
Com - in' for to car - ry me home! But still my soul feels

Com - in' af - ter me, Com - in' for to car - ry me home.
I'm a - com - in' too, Com - in' for to car - ry me home.
hea - ven - ly bound, Com - in' for to car - ry me home.

The chorus alone can be sung in tandem with "When the saints go marching in" (104) or with "All night, all day" (126) as a two-part rouser; brave groups may even attempt all three at once.

104. When the saints go marching in

Oh, when the saints   go march-ing in,   Oh, when the
Oh when the band   be - gins to play,   Oh when the
Oh, when the peo   - ple are set free,   Oh, when the

saints go march-ing in,   Oh, Lord, I want to be in that
band be - gins to play,   Oh, Lord, I want to be in that
peo - ple are set free,   Oh, Lord, I want to be in that

num - ber   When the saints go march - ing in!
num - ber   When the band be - gins to play.
num - ber   When the peo - ple are set free.

Verse 1 can be sung in tandem with "Swing low, sweet chariot" (103) as a two-part rouser. Many
other verses are commonly used as well as these, such as "Oh when the sun begins to shine..."

105. Amen

A - men! A - men! A - men! A - men! A - men!

In this song, as it is usually sung, the leader calls out phrases while the group repeats the "Amen"
chorus. While the actual wordings may vary widely, they often go something like this:

Leader:
1. See the little baby (A-men), lyin' in the manger (A-men), on that Christmas
   morning (A-men, A-men, A-men)
2. See him in the temple... talking with the elders... marvelled at his wisdom...
3. See him by the seaside... talking to the people... healing their diseases....
4. Marching to Jerus'lem... waving palm branches... in pomp and splendor....
5. See him in the garden... talking to the Spirit... In deepest sorrow...
6. Led before Pilate... They crucified him... But he rose on Easter...
7. Alleluia!... He died to save us... Now he lives forever...

106. Where have all the flowers gone?

1. Where have all the flow-ers gone? Long time pass-ing.

Where have all the flow-ers gone? Long time a-go.

Where have all the flow-ers gone? The girls have picked them ev-'ry-one

When will they ev-er learn? When will they ev-er learn?

2. Where have all the young girls gone?... They've taken husbands evr'y one.
3. Where have all the young men gone?... They're all in uniform.
4. Where have all the soldiers gone?... They've gone to graveyards, ev'ry one.
5. Where have all the graveyards gone?... They're covered with flowers, ev'ry one.
6. Where have all the flowers gone?... Young girls picked them, ev'ry one.

Although this song is relatively recent, the form goes back many centuries. In many parts of the world, composers and poets have created "circular-question" songs, which conclude by coming back to the beginning. Pete Seeger based this song on a verse from an ancient folk song, quoted by Mikhail Sholokov in "And Quiet Flows the Don."

107. John Brown's body

John Brown's bod - y lies a - mould-rin' in the grave
John Brown died to put an end to sla - ver - y,
He captured Harper's Fer - ry with his nine-teen men so true, He
The stars a - bove in heav -en are look-ing kind- ly down, The

John Brown's bod - y lies a - mould-rin' in the grave.
John Brown died to put an end to sla - ver - y,
frightened Old Vir-gin - ny 'til she trem - bled thru and thru, They
stars a - bove in heav - en are look - ing kind - ly down, The

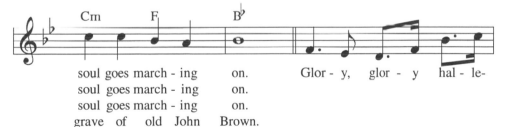

John Brown's bod - y lies a - mould- rin' in the grave, But his
John Brown died to put an end to sla - ver - y, But his
hung him for a trait-or they them-selves the trait - or crew, But his
stars a-bove in heav-en are look- ing kind - ly down, On the

soul goes march - ing on. Glor - y, glor - y hal - le-
soul goes march - ing on.
soul goes march - ing on.
grave of old John Brown.

lu - jah, Glor - y, glor - y hal - le - lu - jah,

Glor - y, glor - y hal - le - lu - jah, His soul goes march - ing on.

108. Joy is like the rain

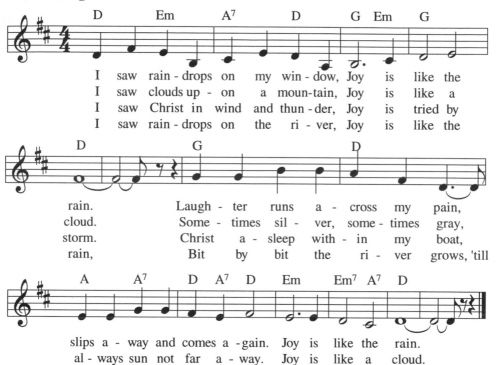

I saw rain-drops on my win-dow, Joy is like the rain.
Laugh-ter runs a-cross my pain, slips a-way and comes a-gain. Joy is like the rain.

I saw clouds up-on a moun-tain, Joy is like a cloud.
Some-times sil-ver, some-times gray, al-ways sun not far a-way. Joy is like a cloud.

I saw Christ in wind and thun-der, Joy is tried by storm.
Christ a-sleep with-in my boat, whipped by wind, yet still a-float. Joy is tried by storm.

I saw rain-drops on the ri-ver, Joy is like the rain,
Bit by bit the ri-ver grows, 'till all at once it o-ver-flows. Joy is like the rain.

Words and music: Sister Miriam Therese Winter

109. Rock-a my soul

Rock-a my soul in the bo-som of A - bra - ham;

Rock-a my soul in the bo-som of A - bra - ham;

Rock-a my soul in the bo-som of A - bra-ham;

Oh, rock-a my soul. So high, you can't get o - ver it;

So low, you can't get un - der it; So wide, you

can't get a - round it; You've got to go in at the door.

110. It's a-me, O Lord

It's a - me, it's a - me, O Lord, stand-ing in the need of

prayer. prayer. Not my broth - er, nor my sis - ter, but it's
Not my preach - er, not my teach - er, but it's
Not my moth - er, not my fath - er, but it's
Not my neigh - bor, not a stran - ger, but it's

me, O Lord, stand - ing in the need of prayer. prayer.

Sing the chorus and each verse twice; use the first ending the first time, the second ending the second time.

111. Loch Lomond

By   yon   bon - nie banks and   by   yon bon - nie braes, Where the
I   mind where we part - ed   in   yon sha - dy glen, On   the
The   wee   bir - dies sing and   the   wild flo -wers spring, And   in

sun   shines   bright on Loch Lo -mond,   Where   me   and my true love were
steep, steep   side of Ben Lo -mond, Where in deep pur -ple hue   the
sun - shine the wa - ters are sleep - ing. But the bro - ken heart   will

ev - er wont to be   On   the   bon - nie, bon - nie banks of Loch Lo - mond.
High -land hills we viewed, And the moon   com - ing   out   in the gloam- ing.
know   no   sec- ond spring And the   world   does not know we are weep - ing.

Oh,   you'll   take the high   road   and   I'll   take   the low   road, And

I'll   be   in Scot - land be - fore   you. But   me   and my true   love will

ne - ver meet a - gain On the   bon-nie, bon-nie banks of Loch Lo - mond.

Though often treated as a happy love song, this is actually a lament. The lovers never expect to see
each other again; the "low road" is the grave.

Words: Lady John Scott

112. We are one in the spirit

We are one in the Spir-it, We are one in the
We will walk with each oth-er, We will walk hand in
We will work with each oth-er, We will work side by

Lord, We are one in the Spir-it, We are
hand, We will walk with each oth-er, We will
side, We will work with each oth-er, We will

one in the Lord, And we pray that all
walk hand in hand, And to-geth-er we'll
work side by side, And we'll guard each one's

u-ni-ty will one day be re-stored And they'll
spread the news that God is in our land,
dig-ni-ty and save each one's pride,

know we are Chris-tians by our love, by our love, And they'll

know we are Chris-tians by our love.

Words and music: Peter Scholtes
Original title: "They'll know we are Christians by our love"

113. This train

This train is bound for glo - ry, this train.
This train don't carry no gam - blers, this train.
This train don't carry no li - ars, this train.
This train is built for speed now, this train.

This train is bound for glo - ry, this train.
This train don't carry no gam - blers, this train.
This train don't carry no li - ars, this train.
This train is built for speed now, this train.

This train is bound for glo - ry
This train don't carry no gam - blers,
This train don't carry no li - ars
This train is built for speed now

Don't ride no - thin' but the righ-teous and the ho - ly
no hy - po - crites and no mid-night ram - blers
no hy - po - crites and no high fly - ers
fast - est train you ev - er did see now

This train is bound for glo - ry, this train.
This train don't carry no gam - blers, this train.
This train don't carry no li - ars, this train.
This train is built for speed now, this train.

In some versions the final line is always, "This train is bound for glory, this train."

Adapted by Woody Guthrie

114. Do Lord

I've got a home in glo - ry land that out - shines the sun,

I've got a home in glo - ry land that out - shines the sun;

I've got a home in glo - ry land that out - shines the sun,

Way be - yond the blue.   Do Lord, O do Lord, O

do re - mem - ber me,   Do Lord, O do Lord, O

do re-mem-ber me,   Do Lord, O do Lord, O

do re - mem- ber me,   Way be - yond the blue.

Words: attributed to Everett George Washington

115. Grandfather's clock

My grand-fa-ther's clock was too large for the shelf, So it
In watch-ing its pen-du-lum swing to and fro, Ma-ny
My grand-fa-ther said that of those he could hire, Not a
It rang an a-larm in the dead of the night, An a-

stood nine-ty years on the floor. It was tal-ler by half than the
hours had he spent while a boy; And in child-hood and man-hood the
ser-vant so faith-ful he found; For it was-ted no time, and had
larm that for years had been dumb; And we knew that his spir-it was

old man him-self, Though it weighed not a pen-ny-weight more. It was
clock seemed to know, And to share both his grief and his joy. For it
but one de-sire, At the close of each week to be wound. And it
plu-ming its flight, That his hour of de-par-ture had come. Still the

bought on the morn of the day that he was born, And was
struck twen-ty four when he en-tered at the door, With a
kept in its place, not a frown up-on its face, And its
clock kept the time, with a soft and muf-fled chime, As we

al-ways his treas-ure and pride; But it stopped short
bloom-ing and beau-ti-ful bride;
hands ne-ver hung by its side;
si-lent-ly stood by his side;

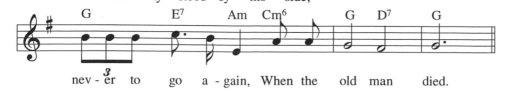

nev-er to go a-gain, When the old man died.

Words and music: Henry Clay Work

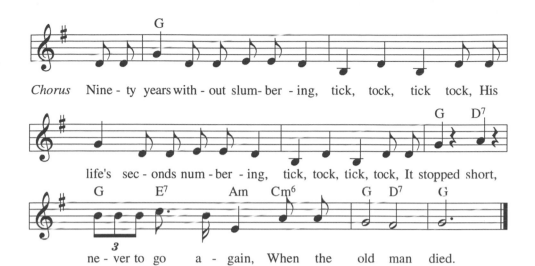

Chorus   Nine - ty years with - out slum- ber - ing,   tick,   tock,   tick   tock,   His

life's   sec - onds num - ber - ing,   tick, tock, tick, tock, It stopped short,

ne - ver to go   a - gain,   When   the   old   man   died.

116. He's got the whole world

1. He's got the whole world in his hands,
2. She's got the wind and the rain in her hands,
3. He's got the tiny lit - tle ba - by in his hands,
4. She's got you and me sis - ter in her hands,

he's got the whole round world in his hands,
she's got the sun and the moon in her hands,
he's got the tiny lit - tle ba - by in his hands,
she's got you and me bro - ther in her hands,

he's got the whole world in his hands,
she's got the wind and the rain in her hands,
he's got the tiny lit - tle ba - by in his hands,
she's got you and me sis - ter in her hands,

he's got the whole world in his hands.
she's   her

5. He's got everybody here in his hands... He's got the whole world in his hands.

117. Lord, I want to be a Christian

Lord, I want to be a Chris-tian in - a my heart, in - a my
Lord, I want to be more lov - ing in - a my heart, in - a my
Lord, I want to be more ho - ly in - a my heart, in - a my
Lord, I want to be like Je - sus in - a my heart, in - a my

heart, Lord, I want to be a Chris - tian in - a my
heart, Lord, I want to be more lov - ing in - a my
heart, Lord, I want to be more ho - ly in - a my
heart, Lord, I want to be like Je - sus in - a my

heart, In - a my heart, In - a my heart, Lord, I
heart,
heart,
heart,

want to be a Chris- tian in - a my heart.

Hampton University Archives, Hampton, Virginia

118. Go tell it on the mountain

When I was a sin-ner, I prayed both night and day, I
And when I was a seek-er, I sought both night and day, I

asked the Lord to help me, And God showed me the way.
asked the Lord to help me, And God taught me to pray.

Go tell it on the moun - tain; Ov - er the hills and

ev - 'ry - where Go tell it on the

moun - tain, That Je - sus Christ is born.

When sung as a Christmas carol:

1. While shepherds kept their watching, O'er silent fields by night
   Behold throughout the heavens, There shone a holy light...

2. The shepherds feared and trembled, When lo, above the earth
   Rang out the angel chorus, that hailed our Savior's birth...

3. Down in a lowly manger, The humble Christ was born,
   And God sent our salvation, That blessed Christmas morn...

Other traditional verses to this old spiritual include:
"When I was a learner..."
"He made me a watchman, Upon the city wall, And if I am a Christian, I am the least of all..."
"And lo, when they had seen it, They all bowed down and prayed, Then travelled on together, To where the Babe was laid..."

119. Oh, freedom!

Oh, free - dom! oh, free - dom! oh, free - dom
There'll be laugh-ing, there'll be laugh-ing, there'll be laugh-ing
There'll be sing-ing, there'll be sing-ing, there'll be sing- ing
There'll be peace, there'll be peace, there'll be peace

o - ver me! (o - ver me) An' be - fo' I'd be a slave, I'll be
o - ver me! (o - ver me)
o - ver me! (o - ver me)
o - ver me! (o - ver me)

bu-ried in my grave, An' go home to my Lord an' be free.

Vespers and closings

The loon calls, the water laps against the rocks, the sun sinks into a crimson horizon. The days have been busy, with much to do, but now we can sit quietly with one another. We can take the time to reflect on what we have done, on what we have learned from each other, on the spiritual currents that run through our community and bind us together.

Sometimes we disperse only for the evening. Sometimes we will go our separate ways, not to meet again for week, a year, forever. Vespers songs, as well as opening us to the spirit in our midst, help us wind down and prepare for departure.

Circles of people begin with words and songs that set the tone for their time together. And when the time comes to close, words and music can again set the tone. We honor the time and the companionship we have had; we honor the spirit that has been among us. Now we move out from our circles, back into the world.

120. Peace of the river

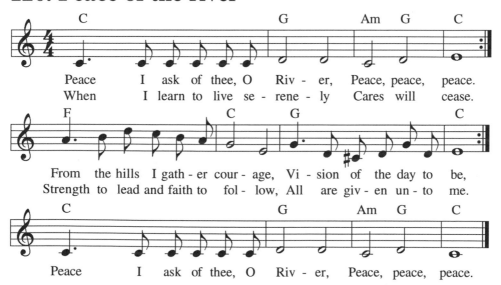

Peace I ask of thee, O Riv - er, Peace, peace, peace.
When I learn to live se - rene - ly Cares will cease.

From the hills I gath - er cour - age, Vi - sion of the day to be,
Strength to lead and faith to fol - low, All are giv - en un - to me.

Peace I ask of thee, O Riv - er, Peace, peace, peace.

Depending on where you live, "forest", "ocean", or "waters" may be used as alternates for "river".

121. Magic penny

Chorus Love is some-thing if you give it a-way,

Give it a-way, give it a-way. Love is some-thing if you

give it a-way, You end up hav-ing more. It's just like a
So let's go dancing 'til

mag-ic pen-ny Hold on tight and you won't have an-y.
the break of day If there's a pi - per we can pay

Lend it, spend it and you'll have so man-y They'll
For love is some-thing if you give it a - way You

roll all o - ver the floor. For
end up hav - ing more. For

Words and music: Malvina Reynolds

122. Let there be peace on earth

Let there be peace on earth And let it be-gin with me.

Let there be peace on earth The peace that was meant to be. With

Original lyrics: God as our Fa-ther Bro-thers all are we.
Alternate lyrics: God as Cre-a-tor, Child-ren all are we.

Let me walk with my bro-ther In per-fect har-mo-ny.
Let us walk with each o-ther In per-fect har-mo-ny.

Let peace be-gin with me, Let this be the mo-ment now.

With ev-'ry step I take, Let this be my sol-emn vow; To

take each mo-ment and live each mo-ment in peace e-ter-nal-

Words and music: Sy Miller and Jill Jackson, 1955

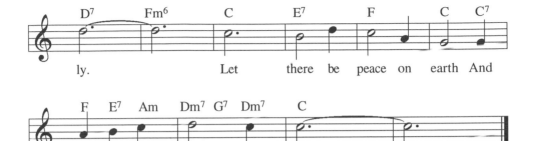

ly.   Let   there   be   peace   on   earth   And

let   it   be - gin   with   me.

In the third and fourth lines on the opposite page, the wordings are alternates. The top line shows the original version, as written; the lower line shows modifications for more inclusive reference.

123. Peace is flowing like a river

Peace	is	flow - ing	like	a	riv	-	er,	flow - ing
Love	is	flow - ing	like	a	riv	-	er,	flow - ing
Heal- ing's	flow - ing	like	a	riv	-	er,	flow - ing
Al - le - lu - ia,	al - le -	lu	-	ia,	Al - le-

out   of   you and   me. — — Flow - ing   out in - to the
out   of   you and   me. — — Flow - ing   out in - to the
out   of   you and   me. — — Flow - ing   out in - to the
lu   -   ia, al - le - lu   -   ia.   Al - le - lu - ia, al - le -

des   -   ert,   set - ting   all   the cap - tives   free.
des   -   ert,   set - ting   all   the cap - tives   free.
des   -   ert,   set - ting   all   the cap - tives   free.
lu   -   ia,   Al - le - lu - ia, al - le - lu.

Words and music adapted by Rev. Carey Landry

124. All my trials Lord

Hush lit-tle ba-by don't you cry, You
riv-er of Jor-dan is mud-dy and cold, It
liv-ing were a thing that mon-ey could buy, You

know your Ma-ma was born to die.
chills the bod-y but warms the soul,
know the rich would live and the poor would die.

All my tri-als, Lord, Soon be

Fine

o - ver. The Too late, my broth-ers,
sis - ters,

After 2nd verse only

Too late but ne-ver mind, All my

tri - als, Lord, Soon be o - ver. If

Although it is almost impossible to trace the origin of most traditional songs, this one is supposed
to have started in the southern USA, then moved through the West Indies and the Bahamas to
become a staple of the folk song movement. In the bridge between verses 2 and 3, sing either
"brothers" or "sisters" as seems appropriate.

125. Pass it on

It on - ly takes a spark to get a fire
What a won - drous time is spring when all the trees are
I wish for you my friend this hap - pi - ness that

go - ing, And soon all those a - round Can
bud - ding, The birds be - gin to sing, The
I've found, You can de - pend on Him, It

warm up to its glow - ing. That's how it is with
flow - ers start their bloom - ing. That's how it is with
mat - ters not where you're bound. I'll shout it from the

God's love Once you've ex - per - i - enced it; You
God's love Once you've ex - per - i - enced it; You
moun - tain top I want my world to know; The

spread His love to ev - 'ry - one; You want to pass it on.
want to sing, it's fresh like spring, You want to pass it on.
Lord of love has come to me, I want to pass it on.

Many groups substitute "God" and "God's" for "Him" and "His" in the interests of more inclusive language. This printed version is, however, the only form authorized by the copyright holders.

Words and music: Kurt Kaiser
Copyright © 1969 Bud John Songs, Inc.

126. All night, all day

All night, all day, an-gels watch-in' o-ver me, my Lord.

All night, all day, an-gels watch-in' o-ver me.

Now I lay me down to sleep An-gels
If I die be - fore I wake An-gels
If I live a - noth-er day An-gels

watch-in' o-ver me, my Lord. Pray the Lord my
watch-in' o-ver me, my Lord. Pray the Lord my
watch-in' o-ver me, my Lord. Pray the Lord to

soul to keep An-gels watch-in' o-ver me.
soul to take An-gels watch-in' o-ver me.
guide my way An-gels watch-in' o-ver me.

The choruses of "All night, all day" and "Swing low, sweet chariot" (103) have been sung together as a two-part song by some groups. Some groups also introduce a kind of descant by having part of the group simply sing "Angels..." holding the A for two more bars while the rest of the group completes the phrase "...watchin' over me."

127. Make me a channel of your peace

1. Make me a chan-nel of your peace: where there is ha-tred
2. Make me a chan-nel of your peace: where there's des-pair in
4. Make me a chan-nel of your peace: It is in par-don-

let me bring your love; where there is in-ju-ry, your heal-ing
life let me bring hope; where there is dark-ness, on-ly
ing that we are par-doned, in giv-ing to all peo-ple we re-

pow'r, and where there's doubt, true faith in you.
light, and where there's sad-ness, ev - er joy.
ceive, and in dy - ing that we're born to e-ter-nal life.

3. O Spir-it, grant that I may nev-er seek so

much to be con - soled as to con - sole,

to be un-der-stood as to un-der-stand, to be

to verse 4

loved as to love with all my soul.

Words: traditional Music: Sebastian Temple

128. Lord of the dance

1. I danced in the morn-ing when the world was be-gun And I
2. I danced for the scribe and the phar - i - see, But
3. I danced on the Sab-bath and I cured the lame. The

danced in the moon and the stars and the sun, And I
they would not dance and they would not fol-low me, I
ho - ly peo - ple said it was a shame. They

came down from heav - en and I danced on the earth, At
danced for the fish - er - men, for James and John, They
whipped and they stripped and they hung me high, And

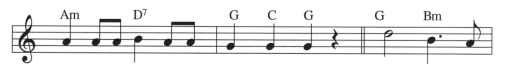

Beth - le - hem I had my birth. Dance, then, wher-
came with me and the dance went on.
they left me there on a cross to die.

ev - er you may be; I am the Lord of the Dance said he, And I'll

Words: Sydney Carter
Music: adapted from a Shaker melody by Sydney Carter

lead you all wher - ev - er you may be, And I'll

lead you all in the dance, said he.

4. I danced on a Friday when the sky tuned black
   It's hard to dance with the devil on your back;
   they buried my body and they thought I'd gone
   but I am the dance and I still go on ...

5. They cut me down and I leap up high:
   I am the life that'll never never die;
   I'll live in you if you'll live in me
   I am the Lord of the Dance, said he...

129. Evening is here now

1. Evening is here now, daylight is fading,
   Deepening shadows herald the night.
   Praise for the day now closing around us;
   Praise the Creator, giver of light.

2. This day has brought us moments of sharing,
   Deeper reflection, knowledge increased;
   Minds have been opened, hopes gently nurtured,
   Friendships extended, new love released.

3. Night is approaching, bringing a stillness
   Into the world around and within.
   This is a time for rest and renewal,
   Waiting the promise morning will bring.

Words: John Ambrose   Music: "Morning has broken"

130. Today

To- day while the blos- soms still cling to the vine, I'll taste your straw - ber -ries, I'll drink your sweet wine. A mil - lion to - mor - rows shall all pass a -way, Ere I for - get all the joy that is mine, To - day.

1. I'll be a dan - dy and I'll be a rov - er You'll know who I am by the song that I sing. I'll feast at your ta - ble, I'll sleep in your clo - ver, Who cares what the mor - row shall bring. To -

2. I can't be con - tent - ed with yes - ter - day's glo - ry, I can't live on prom - is - es win - ter to spring. To - day is my mo - ment and now is my sto - ry, I'll laugh, and I'll cry, and I'll sing. To -

Words and Music: Randy Sparks

131. Amazing grace

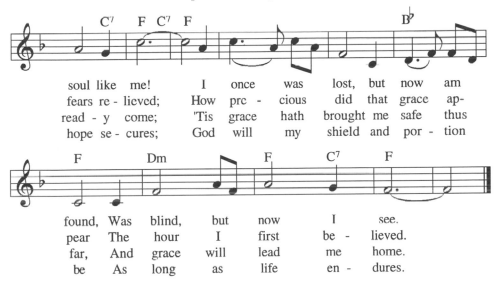

1. A - maz - ing grace! how sweet the sound, That saved a
2. 'Twas grace that taught my heart to fear, And grace my
3. Through man - y dan - gers, toils, and snares, I have al-
4. The Lord has prom - ised good to me, God's word my

soul like me! I once was lost, but now am
fears re - lieved; How pre - cious did that grace ap-
read - y come; 'Tis grace hath brought me safe thus
hope se - cures; God will my shield and por - tion

found, Was blind, but now I see.
pear The hour I first be - lieved.
far, And grace will lead me home.
be As long as life en - dures.

5. When we've been there ten thousand years,
   Bright shining as the sun,
   We've no less time to sing God's praise
   Than when we first begun.

6. Amazing grace! that set me free
   To touch, to taste, to feel;
   The wonders of accepting love
   Have made me whole and real.

John Newton was the captain of a ship carrying slaves to America. During the voyage, he was converted, and immediately took his ship back to Africa where he set his cargo free.

Words : verses 1-4, John Newton; verse 5, John P. Rees;
verse 6, attributed to New York YM Quakers.
Music: early American melody

132. Abide with me

1. A - bide with me; fast falls the ev - en - tide;
2. Swift to its close ebbs out life's lit - tle day;
3. I need thy pres - ence e - v'ry pass - ing hour;

The dark - ness deep - ens; Lord, with me a - bide,
Earth's joys grow dim, its glor - ies pass a - way;
What but thy grace can foil the tempt - er's power?

When o - ther help - ers fail, and com - forts flee,
Change and de - cay in all a - round I see;
Who like thy - self my guide and stay can be?

Help of the help - less, O a - bide with me.
O thou who chang - est not, a - bide with me.
Through cloud and sun - shine, Lord, a - bide with me.

Music: William Henry Monk 1823 - 1889
Words: Henry Francis Lyte 1793 - 1847

133. Red river valley

'Tis   a long time that I have been wait - ing   For the
From this val - ley they say you are go - ing;   I shall
Of - ten think of   the Red Ri - ver Val - ley.   Ver - y
When you sail far a - cross the wide o - cean,   May you

words that you ne - ver would say,   But to - day my last hope it has
miss your bright eyes and your smile.   Far from me you are tak - ing the
lone - ly and sad I shall   be   Do re - mem - ber the heart you are
ne - ver for - get those bright hours That we spent on the banks of the

van - ished, For they say you are go - ing a - way.   Come and
sun - shine That has bright-ened my path for a - while.
break - ing; Pro - mise you will be faith - ful to me.
ri - ver   In the eve - nings a - mong prair-ie flow'rs.

sit by my side if you love me,   Do not has - ten to bid me a-

dieu, But re - mem - ber the Red Ri - ver Val - ley,   And the

one   who has loved   you   so true.

Although this folk song probably started its life in the eastern USA, it has become firmly associated in Canada with Manitoba's Red River.

134. Kum ba yah

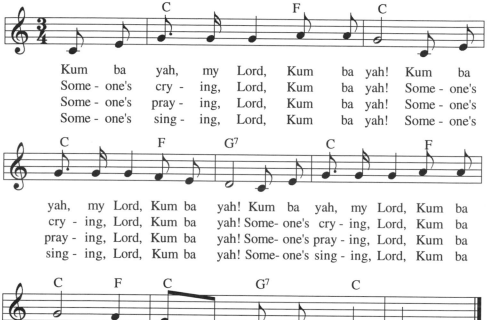

Kum ba yah, my Lord, Kum ba yah! Kum ba
Some - one's cry - ing, Lord, Kum ba yah! Some - one's
Some - one's pray - ing, Lord, Kum ba yah! Some - one's
Some - one's sing - ing, Lord, Kum ba yah! Some - one's

yah, my Lord, Kum ba yah! Kum ba yah, my Lord, Kum ba
cry - ing, Lord, Kum ba yah! Some- one's cry - ing, Lord, Kum ba
pray - ing, Lord, Kum ba yah! Some- one's pray - ing, Lord, Kum ba
sing - ing, Lord, Kum ba yah! Some- one's sing - ing, Lord, Kum ba

yah! O Lord, Kum ba yah!
yah! O Lord, Kum ba yah!
yah! O Lord, Kum ba yah!
yah! O Lord, Kum ba yah!

"Kum ba yah" is an West Indian pidgin-English rendering of "Come by here." As with many songs from the slavery era, it starts as a prayer for help. There is almost no limit to the number of possible verses, but the progression of "crying... praying... singing..." often moves on to "Someone's laughing, Lord..." and "Someone's happy, Lord..." The first verse is often sung as a chorus, or used to conclude the song.

135. Dona nobis pacem

Do - na no - bis pa - cem pa - cem

Do - na no - bis pa - cem

Do - na no - bis pa - cem

Do - na no - bis pa - cem

Do - na no - bis pa - cem

Do - na no - bis pa - cem

Although normally sung as a conventional round, with each of the three groups singing all three parts in sequence, this can also be sung beautifully by dividing into three groups and having each group sing only its own part.

136. Shalom

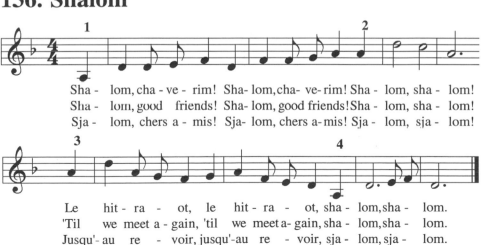

Sha - lom, cha - ve - rim! Sha - lom, cha - ve - rim! Sha - lom, sha - lom!
Sha - lom, good friends! Sha - lom, good friends! Sha - lom, sha - lom!
Sja - lom, chers a - mis! Sja - lom, chers a - mis! Sja - lom, sja - lom!

Le hit - ra - ot, le hit - ra - ot, sha - lom, sha - lom.
'Til we meet a - gain, 'til we meet a - gain, sha - lom, sha - lom.
Jusqu'- au re - voir, jusqu'-au re - voir, sja - lom, sja - lom.

Originally from Hebrew, this song is suitable for singing as a round, in any (or all three) of the languages. Some groups sing "I'll meet you again" instead of "Till we meet again."

137. One tin soldier

Lis-ten chil-dren to a sto - ry that was writ-ten long a - go
So the peo- ple of the val- ley sent a mes- sage up the hill
Now the val- ley cried with an-ger, mount your hors-es, draw your sword,

'bout a king - dom on a moun-tain and the val - ley folk be - low.
ask-ing for the bur-ied treas-ure, tons of gold for which they'd kill.
and they killed the moun-tain peo-ple so they won their just re - ward.

On the moun-tain was a treas - ure bur -ied deep be - neath a stone
Came an an-swer from the king-dom: "With our broth-ers we will share
Now they stood be-side the treas - ure on the moun-tain, dark and red

and the val - ley peo-ple swore they'd have it for their ver - y
all the se - crets of our moun- tain all the rich - es bur -ied
turned the stone and looked be-neath it "Peace on earth" was all it

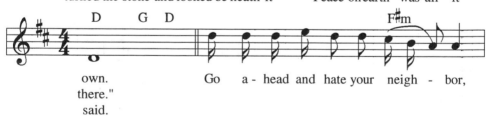

own. Go a - head and hate your neigh - bor,
there."
said.

go a-head and cheat a friend. Do it in the name of heav - en.

Words and music: Dennis Lambert and Brian Potter

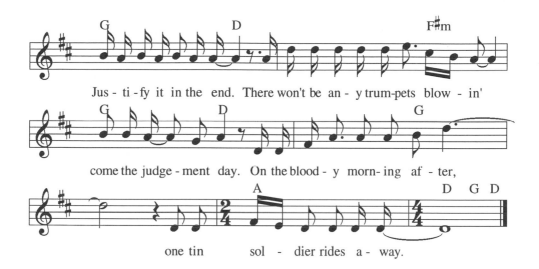

Jus - ti -fy it in the end. There won't be an - y trum-pets blow - in'

come the judge - ment day. On the blood - y morn- ing af - ter,

one tin sol - dier rides a - way.

138. Day is done

Day is done, Gone the sun, From the lake, From the hills,

From the sky. All is well, Safe - ly rest, God is nigh.

This song, also known as "Taps," is commonly used to conclude the day at camp. It is often accompanied by some kind of closing ritual, such as lowering a flag, or greeting each other with handshakes and hugs and "Thanks for the evening, camper!" Near coastal areas, substitute "sea" for "lake."

139. Auld lang syne

Should auld ac - quaint - ance be for - got, And
And here's a hand my trus - ty frien', And

nev - er brought to mind? Should auld ac - quaint - ance
gie's a hand o' thine; We'll tak' a cup o'

be for - got, And days of auld lang syne? For
kind - ness yet For auld lang syne.

auld lang syne, my dear, For auld lang syne; We'll

take a cup o' kind - ness yet, For auld lang syne.

Words: Robert Burns   Music: traditional Scottish melody

140. Go now in peace

Go now in peace, go now in peace. May the love of

God sur - round you ev - 'ry - where, ev - 'ry - where you may go.

Usually sung as a round.   Words and music: Natalie Sleeth

Subject index

First line or title index

When a commonly-used title differs significantly from the first line of the song, the title is shown in italic type.